Preaching
to Skeptics
and Seekers

Preaching to Skeptics and Seekers

Frank G. Honeycutt

Abingdon Press
Nashville

PREACHING TO SKEPTICS AND SEEKERS

Library of Congress Cataloging-in-Publication Data

Honeycutt, Frank G., 1957–
    Preaching to skeptics and seekers/Frank G. Honeycutt.
        p. cm.
    Includes bibliographical references.
    ISBN 0-687-09952-8 (alk. paper)
    1. Preaching to non church-affiliated people. 2. Non church-affiliated
    people—Religious life. I. Title.

BV4235.N65 H66 2001
251—dc21

2001022363

Copyright page continued on page 183.

01 02 03 04 05 06 07 08 09 10—10 9 8 7 6 5 4 3 2 1

In memory of
Bill Hoffmeyer

Friend, colleague,
and Appalachian Trail
hiking companion

1954–1998

Contents

Acknowledgments

If not for the many skeptics and seekers in Washington County, Virginia, who listened and responded to these sermons, this book would not be possible. I am particularly grateful for their honesty, candor, and friendship.

I would also like to thank:

—the people of St. John Lutheran Church, Abingdon, Virginia, who granted me a generous study sabbatical to begin work on the idea for this book;

—the teachers and administrators of the Doctor of Ministry in Preaching program offered through the Association of Chicago Theological Schools (ACTS);

—Gene Copenhaver and Ron Luckey, my campus pastors at Clemson University, who led me into the joy of discipleship as a young adult seeker;

—and my parents, Ruth and Bob Honeycutt, who lovingly handed down an appreciation for religious dialogue, tolerance, and diversity.

Foreword

One of my problems with so-called seeker services and seeker-sensitive churches is that, in my pastoral experience, whatever most people are seeking, it isn't Jesus. We live in a society of omnivorous desire where people tend to grab at everything hoping that they might seize upon something that will give them a good reason to get out of bed in the morning. We are trained to be relentless consumers who think that our lives can be made worthwhile through the acquisition of things. In such a climate, it is too tempting for us preachers to reduce the Christian faith to just another lifestyle option, another means of making basically good people even better, another way to get what you thought you wanted before you wanted Jesus.

Pastor Frank Honeycutt cares about seekers, skeptics, questioners, inquirers, drifters, believers, would-be-believers, and all the rest. He takes as an article of faith that the Christian faith is contagious, meant to be shared. And yet he also cares about the stuff of the Christian faith. Good Lutheran that he is, he knows that when it comes to a specifically Christian response to our need, there is no good news without some bad. Our need ought not to be taken too seriously in the wrong way. Jesus is not the fulfillment of all our desires; he is also a judgment upon many of our desires, the rearrangement of our need.

Frank knows that we are in a double bind as Christians. Matthew 28:19-20 has been laid on our backs:

> "Go therefore and make disciples of all nations, baptizing them in the name of the Father and of the Son and of the Holy Spirit, and teaching them to obey everything that I have commanded you. And remember, I am with you always, to the end of the age."

As followers of Jesus, participants in his assault upon the world, we are to "go" and we are to tell everyone about what has happened to us and the world in Jesus. But we are also to be "baptizing" and we are to be "teaching." The gospel does not come naturally, is neither inherent nor innate. Christians are made, not born.

I like the way Frank reaches out to the unchurched in the sermons in this book. He is a gifted, beguiling interpreter of the Christian faith. He is in conversation with contemporary North American culture, and he has a great gift for seizing upon the artifacts of that culture to get the attention and to win the hearts of contemporary American listeners.

Yet, I like even more the way Frank is about the business of baptizing and teaching. The Christian faith is more than an answer, a solution to a problem, a source of meaning for our lives. It is about taking up a cross, about following Jesus down a narrow, countercultural way that not everyone wants to walk. Frank is willing to risk the loss of some of his listeners, the departure of some of his seekers in order to be honest with them about the cost of discipleship.

Allowing us to peer over his shoulder as he thinks about the challenges of communicating the faith to people, we see a master evangelist at work. Frank begins with theology, but his theology quickly moves him toward people, particularly people who, for one reason or another, are on the fringes of the faith. He allows them to talk, to tell their stories, to object, to offer resistance. He takes them seriously, and engages them energetically, but he also takes seriously the peculiarity of the gospel. Thus, this book is a case study in how pastors ought to lead the church in its missionary, evangelistic task of articulating the faith to those who do not yet have it.

As a preacher, I also enjoy the way that Frank keeps stepping back from his sermons to consider them in his frequent "Response" sections of this book. Here is where the preacher considers listener response, evaluates the sermon, and takes an honest look at himself. Thus Frank Honeycutt becomes a model for those of us who must evangelize on the basis of Matthew 28:19-20. I see this book as a great resource in homiletics classes in seminary, a source of guidance and encouragement for practicing pastors, and well as a guide in Seekers classes in congregations where there are those who are bold enough not just to seek, but to seek Jesus.

It is not easy to be a preacher. It is a challenge to reach out beyond the comfortable boundaries of those who already share the Christian faith with us to engage those who do not yet know, much less follow, a crucified Savior. It is an even greater challenge to preach Jesus. Jesus tells us to go into all the world and teach and preach. Yet what Jesus wants preached and taught is often at considerable odds with the ways of the world. Sometimes our evangelistic efforts fail, not because we failed to preach well, but because we preached Jesus.

Yet, by the grace of God, there is success. God grants us a hearing. The gospel's news has become good news for people who find to their surprise that, in all their seeking, Jesus was seeking them. They have, despite their misgivings as listeners and our mistakes as preachers, heard and believed. Their seeking and searching has found its goal and they are home. To be God's instrument in that homecoming is what the preacher seeks. In preaching to those who seek, we delightedly discover that we have all been lovingly sought and found.

William H. Willimon
Duke University Chapel
September 2000

Introduction

Lord, not you
it is I who am absent . . .
You are the stream, the fish, the light,
the pulsing shadow,
you the unchanging presence, in whom all
moves and changes.
How can I focus my flickering, perceive
at the fountain's heart
the sapphire I know is there?
                                        —Denise Levertov[1]

The American church, at the dawn of a new millennium, finds itself facing a dizzying array of thirsts and theologies among its membership and those who seek to become members of a local congregation. God, the "unchanging presence," is sought by increasing numbers of folk who are dissatisfied with the false promises of materialism and the hollowness of secularism. Levertov's analysis of her own "flickering" spirituality describes so many of us. With the psalmist, our souls thirst for God "as a deer longs for flowing streams" (Ps. 42:1), but one need not take a trip to the Religion/New Age book section of Barnes and Noble to discover the utter plurality and diversity of this thirst.

One author in a past issue of *The Christian Century* whimsically notes that "according to a recent poll, one out of ten Americans believes that Elvis isn't really dead. We now have more Elvis believers than we do Episcopalians. What is God trying to tell us?"[2] In Kevin Smith's controversial film, titled *Dogma*, comedian George Carlin plays a Roman Catholic cardinal who is actually a PR man for the Vatican. He's in charge of changing the depressing image of a crucified Jesus to something a little more palatable for the masses. On the front steps of a local church, the good cardinal initiates a campaign called "Catholicism Wow" which replaces the crucifix with a "Buddy Christ" who winks, smiles, and offers followers a big thumbs-up. In a film in which nothing is off limits, Smith, an active churchgoer, still finds time to lampoon the revisionist, "feel-good" mood sweeping the church these days that attempts to make Jesus more accessible for the average American. We know we want and need something; many, including church leaders, are just not sure exactly what.

Please do not misunderstand this as pastoral lament. Although such a reality is no doubt challenging for the local church (I've heard more than one pastor confess to being overwhelmed by various theological factions wishing to be heard within the same congregation), seekers often bring a liveliness to their quest for God that is often altogether missing in more settled and assimilated members. Even if such people never "join" the church, their presence among us ought to rekindle a sense of mission among the membership, offer renewed opportunities to share the faith, and remind a congregation of a central task: to make disciples of the one we name as Lord. That doesn't happen by luck, osmosis, or lip service. We have a real mission in front of us in a culture that is no longer "Christian." These are exciting times indeed for the church.

In this book I want to explore the role of the sermon in the midst of this wider explosion of spiritual unrest and interest now facing the church. I am convinced that the sermon is not only a bridge for the baptized between Word and table, but also a bridge between street and pew for many secular people, now drawn back to some sort of spirituality, but with a lack of clarity as to what that might mean. In this age of religious diversity and inherent confusion about so many options on the religious menu, the sermon not only nurtures and edifies "the choir," but also clarifies, teaches, and raises issues for possible new disciples who may be making decisions about the faith at the very moment the sermon is delivered. Such a realization is daunting, but real.

Preaching, of course, is certainly not the only way to evangelize, but it may well be the first way. Every Sunday morning, in almost any congregation, there are folk on the fringes of the community wondering if this is the place where Christ might be authentically discovered. This is not to say that the sermon is meant to "impress" in a market economy of church shoppers, or to stand out as a more important component of the liturgy than others. It is to say that the preacher who does not link careful exegesis with the potential of making disciples has wasted a formidable evangelical opportunity every Sunday morning. We are being watched and listened to by thoughtful people who are reconsidering church, or perhaps are arriving for the first time.

With that as my assumption—the formational/discipleship *potential* of the sermon—this book specifically aims to discover how two different but related groups "hear" Sunday preaching from various points of view. Over a two-year period I was blessed to work with twenty-two remarkable people: a group of fourteen friends and acquaintances in our small Virginia town who refer to themselves as either agnostic or convinced atheist (these were not your typical, passively unchurched people!) and a group of eight "returnees" in our parish who have recently found their way back to church life after a long absence. All agreed to come and listen to several sermons spaced over a good chunk of the church year and provide valuable feedback with candid written responses. You will soon meet them in the pages of this book and discover their sometimes unorthodox, often unique, understandings and impressions of Christianity and life in the church, with particular attention given to their perspective as new listeners to preaching.

As we worked together, several interesting questions began to surface. What difference does the sermon make to such people? How do skeptics and seekers "hear" sermons differently from the longtime member? And most important: How might patient listening to the responses of skeptics inform preaching aimed at those just returning to church? I discovered that the two groups have much in common. Indeed, pastors seeking to understand those arriving at our churches for a first or second look (many not "darkening the door" since childhood) must first attempt to enter and understand the world of the skeptic—those who have nothing to do with church life for very clear, often compelling and thoughtful, reasons. Seekers do not just decide to seek Jesus, say, one fine Sunday in Pentecost. They usually come from a period of doubt and intense questioning which does not magically cease as soon as they step through the doors of a church. I want to offer the brazen assumption that pastors cannot really know where seekers are coming from (or what in the world they might need) until we take time to learn where they've been. It is not a waste of time to learn from people who may never set foot inside our churches. To learn from people who are *not* coming, who have given up on any possibility of faith in Christ or life in the church, helps inform and shape our ministry toward those for whom faith is emerging as a real possibility.

A couple of years ago around dusk on Holy Saturday, my daughter Hannah and I came early to the church to prepare the fire and get ready for the Easter Vigil. We peeked in the sanctuary, stared at its beauty for a good while in the fading light, and took in the scent of all those lilies. Hannah said, "Gosh, Daddy, it smells like *heaven* in here." And it did.

Long ago, Thomas the skeptic showed up late for Easter (John 20:19-29). He too smelled something. But it wasn't heaven. Thomas smelled a hoax. He wasn't around when Jesus came through locked doors and stood among his friends. He wasn't around when Jesus gave them the Holy Spirit. He wasn't around for the resurrection rejoicing. He just flat-out missed everything.

That's pretty much the story of my life—absent when the action occurs. In Atlanta stadium once as a young boy, I had my glove ready on the first-base side, upper deck, poised to grab any foul balls. Hank Aaron, my absolute idol (he could've been Jesus), fouled one off in the third inning right in front of us, easily within reach. Unfortunately, I was in the bathroom at the time. Thomas was absent and would not trust the reports of others. He needed to experience the risen Jesus for himself.

I'll bet you know somebody like Thomas. Often they're a lot more intriguing and interesting than a lot of church people who too often give the impression of having everything nailed down—who stop asking questions, stop searching, stop growing. "Religion," suggests Richard Rohr, "has not tended to create seekers or searchers, has not tended to create honest humble people who trust that God is always beyond them. We aren't focused on the great mystery. Religion has, rather, tended to create people who think they have God in their pockets, people with quick, easy, glib answers."[3] The first words out of Jesus' mouth in John's Gospel come in the form of a question. "What are you looking for?" (1:38). I think he assumes we're looking for more than our car keys and perhaps continues to pose this question to modern disciples well into faith maturity. I suspect there is a bit of Thomas inside all serious people of faith. Doubt draws and coaxes us to another place in the journey of faith. As Frederick Buechner puts it: "Without somehow destroying me in the process, how could God reveal himself in a way that would leave no room for doubt? If there were no room for doubt, there would be no room for me."[4]

Notice: How did the other disciples react to Thomas's request to let his "fingers do the walking"? Did they treat him as theological pariah? Make Thomas feel guilty for wanting such tangible proof? Jam evangelism tracts down his throat until he gagged on the Easter syrup? Did they say, "Well, you idiot, will you just swallow our story and get on with your life?" We do have this telling line: "A week later his disciples were again in the house, and Thomas was with them" (20:26*a*). For a full week, Thomas was with this community of believers *as an unbeliever*. He was allowed to ask questions, voice doubts, and wander the fields. There is not a hint of conversion coercion in the text.

The implication is that Thomas could have remained a skeptic in that community for months and even years. Thomas and his doubts were made to feel welcome in the middle of that community, the early church. Belief and doubt lived in peace that week, waiting together on Jesus. I am convinced that Thomas's doubts played a strong role in his eventual belief and trust. "My Lord and my God!" (20:28), his subsequent confession of faith, is perhaps the strongest personal christological assertion about Jesus in the New Testament. Thomas's unrelenting search for God is greeted by a God searching intensely for him. It should not be a surprise that some of the most committed Christians of the past were first committed atheists: C. S. Lewis, Thomas Merton, Dorothy Day, Malcolm Muggeridge, Leo Tolstoy, Albert Schweitzer, Evelyn Waugh, Claire Boothe Luce, and Dag Hammarskjøld, to name a few.

A fair reading of this story might now view the local congregation as a modern paradigm of the mutual waiting between Thomas and that early community. Churches are far too often places of rigid indoctrination rather than open discovery. "Believe like we believe or you're not welcome here," is the message we sometimes send. Churches should be more like seminaries where one is given the invitation to explore God and be formed over blessed time by a tradition steeped in cyclical time and less like a forensic lab where everything is black and white and urgent. Real disciples are rarely formed by threats or guilt. They are formed because a community has decided to take seriously their doubts and questions. This does not require a compromise of what one truly believes. But it does demand openness, vulnerability, humility, and the willingness to spend quite a bit of time with another person in holy conversation. Any evangelism effort short of that is really nothing more than manipulation and trying to beef up the Sunday attendance records.

Intense questions about God, especially offered in the context of a loving congregation, can lead an inquirer to a new level of theological understanding. When Kathleen Norris first returned to church after a long absence and stumbled into a Benedictine abbey, she was surprised and even disappointed to find the monks so unconcerned with her skepticism and frustrations with Christianity. "I had thought that my doubts were spectacular obstacles to my faith and was confused but intrigued when an old monk blithely stated that doubt is merely the seed of faith, a sign that faith is alive and ready to grow."[5] Nora Gallagher puts it another way: "Doubt is to me the handmaiden of faith, its cop, the one that keeps faith straight. To doubt is an indication of freedom and a guard against fanaticism."[6] Are we willing to welcome doubters and seekers and extend the holy hospitality that real evangelism requires? Is it possible to give up this notion that people believe in a moment, all at once? If you ask me, we need lots of Thomases around our churches. He eventually understands Jesus better than anyone else in the story. Not bad for a skeptic.

On any given Sunday, pastors may not encounter the adamant skepticism of those who participated in my first test group. I have come to understand, however, that many seekers who are showing up for worship (but not ready to commit to membership) are in various stages of leaving that radically skeptical world, quite open to an alternative, yet still shaped by the questions of their past. It behooves a preacher to know what those questions are and to allow the lectionary texts to speak freely to the real concerns a seeker brings. God's word is meant for such an encounter. It is resilient enough, strong enough, and playful enough to withstand the scrutiny.

Isaiah put it this way to exiles soon to be liberated by Cyrus of Persia: "So shall my word be that goes out from my mouth; it shall not return to me empty, but it shall accomplish that which I purpose, and succeed in the thing for which I sent it" (55:11). The prophet likens God's word to the life-giving heavenly rain and snow that fall for the refreshment of the earth and the sustenance of all who sow and eat. This divine word will now nourish not only a chosen people, but also *an entire earth* (55:10). This is now a decidedly larger mission for the exiles as they return to Jerusalem than when they left. "My word," says the Lord, "will accomplish this."

It seems a lot to expect in a modern world flooded with words. The modern preacher might be suffering from a failure of nerve in an era where words come cheap. How does biblical preaching transform skeptical people in an age of information overload? Why would somebody want to listen to *these* words when others are so much more attractively packaged? What difference can fifteen minutes a week really make? Why not succumb to the temptation of a "sermon service" and focus one's time on really helping people? A preacher begins to wonder about this pledge to the exiles.

"My word shall not return to me empty." That is the promise. Three full years have passed since my work with fourteen skeptics. No one has had a miraculous conversion, but we still talk about the project and even specific sermons when we happen to meet. They are thinking about these words. Who knows what God will do in the future?[7]

One member of my "returnee" group has yet to join the church, and another who did join is close to inactive. But from private conversations, I know the word is working on them, too. Again, it is not the preacher's job to "save" people and take credit when they come around (or blame when they don't). Our job is to trust this exilic promise from so long ago and trust God to bring people home.

Therefore, one primary task in preaching is to help others see scripture not as holding rabbit's-foot power (we've all played "Bible Ouija" and sought guidance with a random finger) but rather *redeeming* power. In truth, the world does not expect such a God. People rarely make a unilateral, independent choice toward such odd redemption, thus underscoring the need for a redeemed community as the primary context for adult conversion.

> Did God fail to come when I called? Then perhaps God is not a minion. So who is God? Did God fail to punish my adversary? Then perhaps God is not a policeman. So who is God? Did God fail to make everything turn out all right? Then perhaps God is not a fixer. So who is God?[8]

The word changes us, but not as we might expect. Transformation happens, but not according to human timetables or desires. Personal change occurs in a fashion we'd never choose by ourselves. We die and rise in the encounter with the word made flesh, the word finding root in our lives. The Bible calls this conversion, new birth. "Merry Christmas" with a twist. "For the message about the cross is foolishness to those who are perishing, but to us who are *being saved* it is the power of God" (1 Cor. 1:18). Paul suggests that conversion isn't all at once but rather a slow process with many stops and starts. We are converted in layers over time.

This means that biblical preaching will lead seekers towards a series of little deaths and ongoing relinquishments. "Do you not know that all of us who have been baptized into Christ Jesus were baptized into his death?" (Rom. 6:3). That just might be the most radical question in the entire Bible. Therefore, preaching begins at the font and returns there regularly. It is only when we confess "yes" to Paul's question—that is, our assent to death in Christ—that God's divine CPR pumps new life into people washed up on a Red Sea shore. The pulpit is one place where those interested in the faith are invited to consider exactly what is at stake when Jesus is named as Lord. There is no arm-twisting here, only an honest description of what redemption entails. During Lent our catechumens struggle with and are led to answer: "What is dying inside of you? What are you leaving behind?" Inherently baptismal, all good preaching will stick closely to this pattern of dying and rising until with Paul we confess: "It is no longer I who live, but it is Christ who lives in me" (Gal. 2:20).

Here, then, is an obvious but overlooked truth: resurrection works only on dead people. Cracking open these old texts will expose in a person the need for new life whether they choose to deal with that or not. Martin Luther once said, "We are all beggars, it is true." A congregation serious about transformation might also say, "We are all exiles, it is true." It is this *redemptive* word, God's word to the "dead" in Babylon, that "shall not return to me empty." The Western church should not be surprised at the explosion of Pentecost power among Christians of developing nations and the diminished role of faith and discipleship in this hemisphere. God raises up those who have died to all. In America, where we have so much to hold on to, it is not immediately obvious that we need God at all. We usually die slowly and resistantly by degrees—in some cases, perhaps, by cultural suffocation. There's a lot to shed ourselves of in America. This will usually take time. Slowly the old self dies. Slowly the new self is raised. We are continually emerging from the chrysalis. We are born again and again. But first you have to die. And this we resist. As a character in one of Flannery O'Connor's stories puts it: "A man with a good car ain't got no need of redemption."

The preacher's role in this labored transformation is not only to speak of his or her own "death" at times (and signs of such should be obvious by the way the preacher now lives), but also to make sure the power of God's word to kill and raise people is not softened or diminished. Daniel Berrigan once said, "A Christian should be prepared to look good on wood." The gospel is good news, but depending on your perspective such news may actually sound pretty bad. So a central role for the preacher is to get a sense of the message, faithfully speak it, and get out of the way. Death is at work and there may be casualties. One of our new members, a recent returnee to church life who had lived most of her adult life as an atheist, came up to me after the Easter Vigil last year and got it just right when she said, "This Holy Week has been so meaningful for me. So full of emotion. It finally hit me that this is not just about Jesus and his death and resurrection long ago. It's also about *my* dying and rising now."

In some areas of Latin America, baptisms are celebrated in a way that might get reported to the Department of Social Services in this country. At the very least, it shocks our sweet, safe sensibilities of the sacrament. A funeral hymn is sung as the procession moves through the congregation. A father carries a child's coffin and a mother a bucket of water from the family well. A priest carries a sleeping infant wrapped only in a blanket. Father places the coffin on the altar. Mom fills it with water. The priest anoints the child's skin with embalming oil, lowers the infant into the water and says, "I kill you in the name of the Father and of the Son and of the Holy Spirit." "Amen!" shouts the assembly. The priest lifts the child into the air for all to see and says, "And I resurrect you that you might love and serve the Lord."[9]

This basic pattern of death and resurrection needs constant recollection. I'm convinced that Jesus was able to pull off everything he did because his paschal identity was mightily intact: "Jesus, knowing . . . that he had come from God and was going to God, got up from the table" and washed feet and more (John 13:3-4). When Arthur Miller wrote *Death of a Salesman* in 1949, I wonder if he knew how much Biff's tragic line spoken over the grave of his father, Willy Loman, would also characterize so many who lived and died in the next half-century: "The man didn't know who he was." That is true of so many, many people, including church people. In contrast, Jesus' selfless, life-giving death on the cross finds its origin in his utter confidence in who he was—Jesus came from God and was returning there. Knowing such a truth about one's real homeland liberates a child of God to risk life for others. We cannot preach about that enough.

But that alone is not enough. Augustine said somewhere that in Holy Communion "we become what we
receive." God's people, the baptized, become Christ's
body as it is placed in their hands. This is wonderful news
for people who have died in Christ. In this new life, we are
raised to dine with one who says, "Come and have breakfast" (John 21.12). Gordon Lathrop asks, "Does the sermon
say what the shared cup says? Is the sermon full of the
death and life, judgment and mercy that are in Christ?"[10]

Not long ago, our home telephones went dead. We
called the local repairman who showed up and immediately suspected squirrels that had probably gnawed
through the sheath in the cable. He expertly attached
what he called a "resistive fault locator" to the main
phone box on the side of the house. "There's your problem," he said seconds later with a breezy confidence.
"Five hundred fifty-one feet down through those trees."
And not a foot farther. Wouldn't it be great to have such
a handy homiletic device in order to precisely pinpoint
the Word's direction and receptivity? A resistive faith
locator? "There's your problem, pastor. Now just say it."

Unfortunately, too many pastors stand in the pulpit
with just such an air of confidence and surety. Such pre-
cision is not how I understand our preaching task. One
priest speaks on behalf of his parishioners who want at
least this much from his sermons:

> Don't make promises God doesn't keep. Account
> for the shaky ground and patches of quicksand.
> Don't deny our disappointments or turn away from
> our broken hearts. Explain the beasts lying in wait,
> the damaged goods that can't be fixed, the trouble
> in the streets. Show us God in the horrors hidden
> under cover of night and the prayers that don't get
> answered. Make your words equal to our predica-
> ment. Give us faith as wild as the world. Describe
> that and we'll hang on every word.[11]

A preacher who stands between font and altar with a Bible in hand should never run out of words, no doubt. But they aren't just any old words. These are admittedly odd words that lead to our continual drowning and reviving. Sometimes it seems like hit or miss. But we have this promise. These are the very words that will not return to God empty. Words that have the power to change.

Sometimes I think of my favorite Wendell Berry poem, "Creation Myth," before sitting down to write a sermon. It is a warm summer's night, well past bedtime, in the Appalachian hills. Bill, "who had got up to cool himself," is leaning against the door jamb of the house, "thinking and smoking." McKinley, Bill's brother, has been away most of the night and now heads home through the pasture and down by the dark woods. "Not a star shone. Not a window." The darkness is so complete that McKinley loses his bearings and completely misses the house.

> . . . Amused, Bill smoked
> his smoke, and listened. He knew where
> McKinley was, though McKinley didn't.
> Bill smiled in the darkness to himself,
> and let McKinley run until his steps
> approached something really to fear:
> the quarry pool. Bill quit his pipe
> then, opened the screen, and stepped out,
> barefoot, on the warm boards. "McKinley!"
> he said, and laid the field out clear
> under McKinley's feet, and placed the map of it in
> his head.[12]

Here is Isaiah's (and the preacher's) hope: a single word can create a whole new world in the mind of the listener. For some the geography of faith is more circuitous and demanding. It's easy to get lost. "Thomas!" called Jesus once upon a time. He "laid the field out clear under

[Thomas's] feet, and placed the map of it in his head." The world of faith is created not when we jam theological propositions down another's throat. Faithful people are created when we hear the voice of Jesus calling our names. Thomas believed, in part, not because he was bullied but because he was accepted, skepticism and all— loved into being by a Lord whose Word keeps coming, calling, creating in even the darkest of nights.

This book attempts to learn from skeptics and seekers through the rather narrow lens of the sermon. Their candid responses to a series of sermons from the Sunday lectionary will assist readers of this book who work with seekers on a regular basis and all pastors who wish to be more sensitive to their regular presence wherever Christians gather. Small groups of parishioners from evangelism teams or those who welcome new members and are responsible for a local Christian formation process might also benefit from reading this book together.

Eight printed sermons are offered here, almost exactly as they were offered on eight Sunday mornings over a two-year period. Printed sermons, of course, are not the same as the real thing. I do not include these as sermonic "jewels" but as valuable parameters for the shape of the theological responses that follow. In the course of the book, the reader will get to know several skeptics and seekers of my acquaintance and how these people process regular Sunday preaching from their unique points of view. It is my hope that you will try to listen to these sermons with their ears. In doing so you will perhaps discover some of the seekers from your own locale in these very pages. I hope you will also discover several homiletical strategies for regular sermon preparation that appreciates the important connection between preaching and adult spiritual formation.

Therefore, this book will also try to probe into a seeker's

past as much as possible in order to inform the crafting of sermons that matter mightily in the faith development of new Christians. Sermons cannot convert all alone. But they can play a vital role in ushering a seeker into the hands of a loving Christ whose pattern of dying and rising all baptized people inherit. To again use Levertov's imagery, preachers are given a weekly opportunity to help focus "the flickering faith" of the modern seeker toward the heart of the baptismal "fountain." Perhaps this is the most we can hope for in a sermon: to assist a seeker in taking another tentative step down the path toward faith, further into the heart of this fountain of death and life. Many steps make up a journey. If one sermon leads a seeker to take another step, it has been well worth our time.

Section I

CHAPTER ONE

Sermons and the Secular Ear[1]

It would take an idiot to believe in God, if you keep
your eyes open in the world today. You can go
ahead and believe in anything you want to believe
in, but if you think about it, it's really a stupid kind
of religion. This guy dies on a cross, a man dies
nailed to a cross, it's almost like, "Let's think of the
craziest thing we can think of. A frog jumps over a
turtle, let's make a religion out of that." Actually
they did: Buddhism. But Buddhism makes more
sense to me than either Christianity or Judaism. In
fact, I would be a Buddhist if it weren't for Richard
Gere.
     —*Kinky Friedman, novelist and musician*[2]

Frederick Buechner suggests that there are some agnostics who are "like the bear who didn't know what was on the other side of the mountain." They just never bothered to look very hard for God. "There are other agnostics," he says, "who have taken many pains. They have climbed over the mountain, and what do you think they saw? Only the other side of the mountain. At least that was all they could be sure of. That faint glimmer on the far horizon could have been just Disneyland."[3]

If this book proposes to discover the relationship between preaching and adult formation (ongoing conversion), it seems wise to back up a bit. Adults new to the faith in our parish are returning to our congregational "catechumenal process," an eight-month period of reflection that parallels the rhythms of the church year, finds its origins in the historic catechumenate of the early church, and culminates in adult baptism or baptismal

reaffirmation at the great Easter Vigil.[4] Participants
engage in open inquiry, write a spiritual autobiography,
practice Lenten disciplines, share in community service,
and discern their spiritual gifts. In order to understand
more completely how these returnees were hearing sermons it seemed prudent to learn more of the world they
had just left: the world of the skeptic. How might the sermonic ear of a convinced atheist compare with that of a
recently baptized adult? Could I persuade a group of
atheists, agnostics, and those in-between who live in our
small town to come to church, listen to the sermon, and
respond without feeling uncomfortable? If so, I might
learn from them about the world our adult catechumens
had recently come from and discern specific issues that
sermons could profitably consider and address. This
would differ from taking a broad look at the
"unchurched" who stay away for unclear reasons. I
wanted honest feedback from those who intentionally
rejected Christianity for very specific reasons.

I am not sure how I've come to know so many agnostic friends. Maybe they're a relief from church routine.
Maybe it stems from my camp counselor days when the
most convinced atheist I've ever known held a frightened autistic child in his arms at three in the morning
and asked me, "If Christians thank God for a beautiful
day, shouldn't they also praise the Lord for hurricanes?"
It was not difficult to cipher his point. We've corre-
sponded for over twenty years now, exchanging fat
ten-page letters, this relationship clarifying my faith by
careful, measured apologetics more than any seminary
classroom ever could. One cannot fake the faith with a
friend who claims he would "chase God down with a
pitchfork" were the Almighty to appear on the road one
fine day. For years now I've been intrigued with why
some believe so passionately and others reject Christianity

entirely. Perhaps there is part of me that dances along that tortuous but ultimately creative line between faith and unbelief. According to Peter Berger, this may not be a bad place to land theologically. "The modern pluralistic situation," he says, "creates anxieties and tensions. It is possible to escape from them in opposite directions. One escape is into a false certainty. The other into an attitude that despairs of any possible access to truth."[5] After all, one would have to be oblivious to the lion's share of the Psalms to miss the heartfelt reserve of those who have truly searched for God but still can't say the creed on Sundays with a straight face. "Lord, I believe; help my unbelief!" (Mark 9:24).

Annie Dillard writes:

> Since sand and dirt pile up on everything, why does the world look fresh for each new crowd? As natural and human debris raises the continents, vegetation grows on the piles. It is all a stage—we know this—a temporary stage on top of many layers of stages, but every year a new crop of sand, grass, and tree leaves freshens the set and perfects the illusion that ours is the new and urgent world now. In every arable soil in the world we grow grain over tombs. Living things from hyenas to bacteria whisk the dead away like stagehands hustling between scenes. To help a living space last while we live on it, we brush or haul away the blowing sand and hack or burn the greenery. We are mowing the grass at the cutting edge.[6]

Although Dillard is a Christian and an active church-goer, her unflinching look at the world also fuels the theological posture for more than one agnostic I have known. Perhaps thoughtful agnostics can become for the church the collective "Preacher" in Ecclesiastes that we most need to hear, who looks at the world with eyes wide open and somehow still believes even in a world of much vanity. "All has been heard. Fear God, and keep his commandments; for that is the whole duty of everyone" (12:13). God must indeed hear a lot. The road where the gospel is truly experienced and the Word truly preached is never all sweetness and light, "an urn of long-stemmed roses and baby's breath to brighten up the front of the church, Jesus as Gregory Peck."[7] Agnostics and their doubts have much to teach Christians who sometimes worship an idol of certitude that even Jesus didn't entirely live up to (Mark 15:34).

I thought of fifteen friends and acquaintances to invite. All but one accepted. "I promise I am not out to convert you," said an early letter. "No one from St. John will phone, visit, come to your house on a bicycle, or otherwise harass you in any way." My "skeptics test group" (as they eventually called themselves) included a legal secretary, child advocate, farmer, college professor, attorney, therapist, dancer/signmaker, guidance counselor, community action coordinator, surveillance expert, potter, paralegal, and two weavers. Most at least knew about each other before the project began. Soon they were sitting together in worship and meeting for brunch afterward. I apparently had created a support group.

The group wrote reams in response to my surveys. These were not people who stayed away from worship for unclear reasons. These skeptics had thought a great deal about God, Jesus, and church and were eager to write about their rejection or doubts about all three. Their responses from September through January totaled close to one hundred pages. One of my first survey questions touched a nerve of honesty that remained throughout: "Could you share why Christianity and its expression through a local congregation is not an option for you at this time?"

I have never had the opportunity to see the Christian philos-

ophy, no matter how liberal, in any terms other than the ones that describe people as being obliged to be in their place with God on top ruling over and judging them. Women have historically been at the bottom of this pile. For the past ten or eleven years I have been practicing a modern interpretation of old European shamanistic traditions.

To date I have not found a particular religious group that did not contain some sort of "hidden" bigotry. I always thought "Christians" were supposed to love and care for all people but I have seen too many so-called Christians categorize certain segments of humanity and look down upon them. Another thing that bothers me is the literal acceptance of the Bible as the actual word of God. The story of the Virgin Mary is so extreme to me. Having a science background, I just can't accept this.

I do not believe in a supreme being. I do believe that there are forces, relationships among matter, and modes of energy that we do not yet understand scientifically, but I see no reason that any of the forces in the universe are deserving of the labels "all knowing," "all loving," or "all powerful." I am deeply troubled by pain and suffering in the world and believe that Christianity has no explanation for its God's lack of intervention.

Religion doesn't compute due to my background in math and science. I question everything until I understand and this seems to anger theologians. I believe in the power of the mind.

I find little spiritual fulfillment in the church services of organized religion. The structure is authoritarian—we are being preached at from someone standing above us. There is little or no emotional or physical contact with others attending the service—we sit in straight rows looking at the back of someone's head. I know I need a spiritual community. But I don't think I can find it in organized religion.

I was increasingly disheartened by the gap between [church] teachings and practices. My [childhood] church's failure to take an active, Bible-based stand against the Vietnam War and war in general was probably the last straw. I do feel somewhat spiritually inert and undeveloped because of the lack of a true community in which to test, extend, and develop my belief system.

[Upon leaving the church] I discovered a great increase in what Walker Percy calls the sovereignty of personal experience. Feelings, thoughts, sensations and experiences did not have to be subjected to the grid of religious and tribal approval.

I am a very eclectic person. I find some major flaws (as well as strengths) in Christian philosophy. Also, I dislike ceremonies in general.

Between the ages of 17 and 20 I came to the conclusion that my understanding of the world I inhabit did not include that identity taught in Christian churches, though it continues to include a profound respect for Jesus and many religious teachers. Sometimes I wish I were in a church so I could criticize. I think Christianity suffers from an over-reliance on the Old Testament and the hatreds of Paul.

I chose not to continue in church once my parents gave me a choice. I found little of value in the content of services. I have much more of a philosophical attitude towards faith, spirituality and belief. The repetition and ritual of services don't do much for me.

I just don't feel a need to attend church. I don't know if there is a God or if the story of Jesus is true. I hope so. But I just don't think it matters. What is important is "goodness and love and the possibility of making the world a better place." But I miss the music of the church.

I am not a believer. I am not comfortable with the concept of faith. I am also uncomfortable with many people who profess Christianity and lead hateful and even evil lives. I see no need to believe in God or an organized belief system in order to lead a quality life.

Many aspects of church I find appealing, but I also find the theology harder and harder to swallow. I used to ignore the parts I didn't believe and tried to concentrate on what I did believe, but I felt like a hypocrite.

I do not consider myself a Christian, as I do not worship Christ. I believe that I can lead a good life, caring for self and others and doing as much good and as little harm to others and the earth as much as possible without being a [church] member.

Such honesty was refreshing. This would be a nice ego check for a pastor used to receiving mostly compliments after the service: "Nice sermon, pastor. You really spoke to me today. Interesting angle on the good Samaritan." No such courtesies (praise the Lord) would be forthcoming from this group. Among my favorite responses from that autumn: "My impression of sermons in general is that they are didactic, boring, patriarchal, condescending, undemocratic monologues which occasionally reach levels of relevance and inspiration." Bless you, my son. A pastor could look high and low and never find a church member to say that at the door! I had the group I was looking for.

I invite you to read the four sermons that follow from the perspective of a friend or acquaintance who has given up on Christ, the church, or both. Talk back to the sermon through the words and experience of your friend. Perhaps take issue with what you read from the reality of the "skeptic" in you (this might especially be fun for pastors who are used to giving all the orthodox "answers" for their congregations!). Each sermon will be followed by a short reflection explaining my own homiletical choices and rationale for engaging the biblical text. I will then allow the skeptics to speak, offering their responses in a mode that is as unedited as possible. Again, my assumption is that skeptics and seekers have much in common and that past passion for unbelief can be creatively used in the process of ongoing conversion of a new Christian. At the conclusion of these four sermons, I will offer a summary section for those who wish to cultivate relationships with skeptics and draw from their doubt for purposes of regular Sunday preaching.

CHAPTER TWO

Table Manners in the Kingdom of God

A Sermon for the Thirteenth Sunday After Pentecost

But when you give a banquet, invite the poor, the crippled, the lame, and the blind. (Luke 14:13)

I was at the Johnson City Medical Center a couple of Tuesdays ago, and Michael John Gifford was eating a late lunch. He was there for the latest in a series of sixty-hour chemotherapy treatments that are helping him fight the reality of childhood leukemia, which for Michael John is now officially in remission. But every other weekend for six months he will be in Johnson City. It's been a long summer for a not-quite-two-year-old and his parents.

Anyway, it was lunchtime there on the pediatric oncology wing. Michael's dad and I got him strapped into the high chair, secured bib and tray, and here came the food. It looked like pretty ordinary fare to me—some green beans, a slice of cheese pizza, and a cup of applesauce. Pretty ho-hum stuff. But *au contraire*. Michael John picked up one of those green beans with the care a priest might take in lifting a chalice toward heaven. He popped it into his mouth, rolled it around a bit, cackled loudly, and then declared: "HOT BEAN!" I've never seen food bring such delight. This little guy was having some sort of epicurean epiphany from a lowly vegetable. And it was certainly lost on me. So he grabbed one from his bowl, wanting to share the bounty maybe, and said, "HERE, FRINK. HAVE HOT BEAN!" And I did. Several.

And then he turned to his dad. All present were going to share in this feast. "JOHN EAT SAUCE!" he commanded.

So we all sat there and ate green beans and applesauce for a good half-hour; even got seconds from down the hall. It's been a long time since I've savored and lingered over food in such a way, commenting on its texture and shape and warmth. We who often eat our meals in such haste, with so little regard for where food comes from, lacking time to contemplate the wondrous mystery of how it grows, can take a cue from Michael John. Hot beans made him happy. No theologian could have better expressed the bliss that food brought him, or the joy of a shared meal.

Have you ever noticed how often Jesus is eating in the Gospels? The man is constantly sitting down at table with somebody, no less than ten times in the Gospel of Luke. Most religious art depicts Jesus as a skinny wisp of a man but if you consider all these times he's chowing down, he may have more accurately resembled somebody like Burl Ives in need of a cholesterol checkup. I suppose he just walked it all off. And, Jesus ate with anybody. He ate with rich and poor, the reputable and the shady, the powerful and the nobodies. Jesus' eating habits made people nervous. In fact, the first serious accusation against Jesus was not that he was some sort of political revolutionary. Do you remember the gripe? "This man is a glutton and a wine-bibber who eats with tax collectors and sinners." A chow-hound and a drunk who mixed with ne'er-do-wells. Truth is, you could make a pretty good case that Jesus was crucified because he ate lunch with the wrong people one time too many. It was offensive to people that Jesus would have so little regard for social class, cultural propriety, and plain old table manners. Jesus was probably killed over his eating habits.

Once when Jesus was invited over to the home of a prominent religious leader to have a bite on the sabbath, "they were watching him closely." They should have watched him even closer. For you can't take Jesus anywhere. Jesus gets a dinner invitation and do you see what happens? He proceeds to offend everybody in the place. First, he gives advice to the snobby guests who are trying that old whistling-while-looking-up-in-the-air trick as they subtly sidle over to the best seats. Jesus, who was Mr. Congeniality in his high-school yearbook, says: "The proper place for a guest is at the bottom, the lowest place." Jesus has brought a lesson plan about humility into a blue-blood gathering. The nerve. I'm confident that people sought him out for more advice later at the hors d'oeuvre table.

But, the cheekiest part of the story is when he turns to his host, and challenges the guest list! Is this gratitude? Are these the manners his mother taught him? He may as well have thrown his napkin down and said in disgust, "This pot roast stinks!" He does say this: "When you're planning a lunch or dinner, don't invite people you know well or want to impress, because they're just going to invite you back and call it square. But when you give a feast, invite the poor, and those who are laid up, and people who can't get around well or who can't even see. See them in your lives for a change. And you will be blessed." And you could have heard a pin drop in that place, because all who were at that meal were fortunate and had connections; they had health insurance and savings accounts. They were all the same, really. Jesus was a threat to their uniformity. Their way of life. And ours.

Annie Dillard writes these words in an essay about the Gospel of Luke: "This Bible," she says, "this ubiquitous, persistent black chunk of a best-seller, is a chink—often the only chink—through which winds howl. When I was a child, the adult members of Pittsburgh society advverted to the Bible unreasonably often. What arcana! Why did they spread this scandalous document before our eyes? If they had read it, I thought, they would have hid it. They did not recognize the lively danger that we would, through repeated exposure, catch a dose of its virulent opposition to their world. Instead they bade us study great chunks of it, and think about those chunks, and commit them to memory, and ignore them."[8]

"Invite the poor, the crippled, the lame, and the blind." I must confess that when I invite people over for a meal, the folk that Jesus describes are normally absent. I invite friends. Chums. It's an embarrassment to place this verse next to most dinner parties I've thrown. What does it mean that we live most of our lives with friends who largely have the same income, educational level, same general interests, and pretty bright opportunities for the future? Someone once said that an easy litmus test to check whether you're following Jesus is to look at his close friends and then look at your own. More than anything else, this comparison reveals our real commitment to Jesus and the mission of his church.

There are a wide variety of opinions as to how to help the poor and unfortunate. Some suggest increased funding for social programs; others say job training is essential with a gradual lessening of public assistance. Some say the poor need this. Others say they need that. Jesus' advice cuts across all political rhetoric. Here he doesn't say to help anybody at all. He says to eat with these people. Start a relationship. Have a feast. Make new friends.

Something happens when we share food with another. When we eat a meal together. When Michael John gave me a HOT BEAN the other day in Johnson City, something passed between us, even though he's only two and I'm forty-one, an age when it's hard to change much or notice new things. He reminded me of this: Meals matter. Even people we have come to despise look lovelier over food. It is nothing short of holy mystery when we sit at table with one another.

Before he died, Jesus did a very strange thing. He did not say, "Go get a bunch of laws changed and bend the wills of the powerful." He didn't say, "Be content with hanging out with your own kind." And he didn't say, "Don't forget to give Christmas baskets once a year to the less fortunate." He didn't say any of those things. Before he died, he took some bread and a cup of wine, and he passed that food around the table and said, "Do this in order to remember me." Do *this*? There are lots of things he could have said in those last hours, but he chose to pass on a meal. For all our shortcomings—for our silence when we should speak up and our churchy chatter when we should be listening to Jesus—this is one thing the church does quite well. We offer a meal each week. Anyone who walks through the door is welcome to kneel and eat and share. Make no mistake. We have a lot of work to do in passing out invitations. The Lord's Supper is not a private meal. Not just a "me and Jesus" thing. It is the place from which we do mission; from which we rise and ask, *Who's not here?* It may be the only place left in our culture where God has any hope of creating the type of community Jesus describes in this lesson. Over a meal. Imagine that.

Downtown behind the old black Virginia Creeper train engine, behind the housing authority and the bike rental shop, a small stream carries the refuse from the streets of Abingdon after a hard rain. It's not the cleanest of places, but for some reason I like to go there with my son, and we throw stones in or pretend to fish. There is a large rock on one side of the stream that has created a small sluice, a little waterfall, through which the stream flows.

The rock catches the refuse, lots of it; the runoff after a downpour—soft drink bottle labels, drinking straws, candy wrappers. Trash, basically.

I am drawn to this place, I think, because it's what the church might look like in time, the way he intended it to look: water from a font bringing the broken and the discarded and the forgotten to the rock that is Jesus—the man who invites and forever changes the way we throw parties.

Response to the Sermon

I believe it was Martin Luther King, Jr., who pointed out that Sunday at 11:00 A.M. is the most segregated hour of the week. He was, of course, speaking of racial segregation in the 1960s. Many maintain that now it's easier to evangelize across race than class. Maybe that's why Jesus' words in Luke 14 concerning table manners in the kingdom of God strike many church members as among the most radical statements he ever uttered. These verses should certainly leave us uncomfortable with the "Homogeneous Unit Principle" espoused by many church growth experts. Jesus rarely stuck with his "own kind." If anything, he was about the unpopular business of dismantling the social, physical, and economic barriers that separate God's people and into which we neatly (unthinkingly, after a point) find ourselves. His methods, though, surprise us. They center around food.

In this sermon, I tried to get our congregation to see two main things: (a) The people we eat with in large measure determine the true parameters of the ongoing, genuine care we are able (willing?) to extend to them. Jesus is talking about a relationship in this text, not charity; and (b) If the main meal of the church is Eucharist, then we must begin to see such meals as more than "me and Jesus" forgiveness time. I wanted to make clear connections between Jesus' radical hospitality and the feast of victory that we celebrate at the Lord's altar. If there is no connection here, members can probably forget trying to do mission and evangelism "out there" with anyone but their own kind.

This sermon made a strong connection with almost every member of the skeptics test group. Many people mentioned a strong desire to make a difference in the world and break down class distinctions that keep us apart. All were drawn to the idea of food and eating together as an approach to this. One respondent summed up the thoughts of several: "[This sermon provided] some insight into how insulated my life is. I work with and for poor people, but I don't socialize with any of my client community. I'm not sure how I feel about this, but the sermon will have me thinking about it."

Although Holy Communion has much homiletical potential in pointing people toward a visible manifestation of what Jesus was talking about in Luke 14, the same respondent was not convinced when I used the Lord's Supper as an illustration of radical inclusion and feeding: "You said that the church provided a meal each week. I would merely point out that communion isn't much of a meal and one must meet certain requirements in order to be invited to participate." Ouch.

Revealed in the responses to this sermon was a longing for community that would truly embody the inclusion Jesus commands (in fact, participants regularly expressed their high admiration for Jesus in this regard), but also a candid confession and valid indictment that most congregations are nowhere near these teachings themselves. Most mainline churches minister well *to* the poor and others Jesus says to invite, but few are actual members. John Alexander, former editor of *The Other Side*, offers this scathing insider's view of the church:

"It's not overwhelmingly obvious that ordinary Christians bear a whole lot better fruit than secular people. When I'm feeling grim, it seems to me that average Christians are about as likely to join the Mafia as to commit themselves seriously to living out the radical nature of Jesus' teaching."[2]

This suggests that the sermon can never be separated from the Christian community that listens to the sermon. Church members sometimes miss this basic truth. My group of outsiders sniffed this out quickly. What kind of people is the gospel producing? "Don't look at the church, look at Jesus," is one way I've heard it defensively put. This won't wash for people looking for an authentic community that names Jesus as Lord. Preaching to outsiders without real transformation occurring in members' lives soon becomes a speech saluting a dead hero from the past. Those in my test group were genuinely interested in the type of ministry described by Jesus in this passage. This appears to be a real possibility for faithful conversation. They are also interested in *seeing* genuine examples of how such radical inclusion of the poor, lame, maimed, and blind are part of the practical, daily rhythms of congregational life.

One respondent summed up nicely the limits of sermons that fail to evoke community transformation: "Sometimes a sermon presents an interesting idea, but basically it is a way for a minister to tell us what we are doing wrong, and how God and/or Jesus would want us to amend our behavior. This doesn't mean much to me." Another said similarly, "I worry that people are satisfied to hear you talk about these points." This response echoed one who said, "I would have liked to have heard more about how we as families and congregations can bridge the gap." One skeptic was even more pointed: "I've generally found sermons to be boring and unmoving. At times I've been happy to hear a social justice message integrated into the sermon, but I don't believe sermons are an effective way to move people to social action—or, for that matter, any type of action."

Preaching must be faithful to the spirit of Jesus and his admonition to follow in his way. But the community that grows out of Sunday worship must also become visibly different over time. "Why do you call me 'Lord, Lord,'and do not do what I tell you?" asks Jesus of his disciples (Luke 6:46). "You shall know the truth, and the truth shall make you odd," said Flannery O'Connor, paraphrasing John 8:32.

This is why preaching that hopes to help form such a visible community must be boldly sacramental. I firmly believe that baptism and Eucharist are two of the last regular celebrations left in our world where guests are admitted regardless of color, health, gender, or wallet. I am fortunate to preach in a community where weekly communion is celebrated and a large, cross-shaped baptismal font with flowing water is at the door where worshipers enter the sanctuary. What other group *besides* the church builds membership this radical way? Sermons grounded between font and table point to the countercultural reality that God is bringing forth through water, wine and bread. It is not the preacher's words that transform the community but this Word "becoming flesh" in the lives of church members. In baptism, our outward differences melt. At table, our common hungers are exposed. Preaching should make these connections for listeners, liberating the sacraments from a narrow, individualist interpretation to help parishioners ask, "Who's not here?" Community homogeneity cannot long be tolerated by those who understand what their dunking means and their eating implies.

This theological posture of preaching between font

and table, calling forth the work that God is doing and has done in the life of the community, cannot be over-stated. Unless we are clear about this a preacher runs the risk of sounding like a paid whiner. "The presence of Christ at the holy table," says Charles Rice, "does not admit just any kind of preaching. Rather, if we follow Luther (and Barth after him), just as Jesus Christ is host of the Eucharist, only Christ is, finally, the true preach-er."[3] Unless we dare to say something so audacious and shocking, the preacher quickly runs into problems with the issue of authority. "Who is she to tell us that, any-way?"

One skeptic in my test group broached this issue nice-ly: "[Sermons are] fraught with a very large problem: the apparent authority of the person delivering the sermon as she describes what she believes to be the 'Truth.' I don't believe that I recall ever hearing a sermon in which the speaker has concluded by saying, 'Well, these ideas are just my opinions, of course. Your ideas may be quite divergent, but still just as valid.'" Another participant raised issues of authority by telling me that "wearing priestly robes turns me off. I believe that everyone should be his/her own priest and that, if we are open to it, Michael Gifford [the "hot bean" boy] is every bit as capable of teaching us as you are."

This issue of authority surfaced early on with the skep-tics who responded to these sermons. Jesus himself, of course, faced regular questions of a similar nature. "By what authority are you doing these things, and who gave you this authority?" ask the chief priests and elders (Matt. 21:23). Why *do* Christians give Jesus so much authority in our lives? Why is *he* our central teacher and spiritual guide rather than somebody else? Isn't it odd that Christians give their lives over to a man with no cre-dentials, someone unwilling to explain himself clearly to others, a man who rarely answered a question head-on? The man whom most of us wouldn't give a second hearing for lack of accreditation were he to stand before us in the flesh today is the one we call Lord and Savior. The skeptics in my test group would at least like to see the guy's driver's license and do a background check. "Jesus is a great moral teacher," says one Christian, defensively. Well, so is the Dalai Lama.

One of the big reasons I trust Jesus is that he invites me on a spiritual journey to discover the living God. Jesus doesn't spell it all out for me. He leaves things open-ended, even ambiguous and foggy. He refuses to be an "authority" whose book we can buy and whose "Five Points to Eternal Happiness" we can listen to at a lecture downtown, signing autographs afterwards. Religion is all too often an exercise in listening to some accredited, authorized, ordained big-whig (like a pastor, I suppose) tell you about God. Which is okay up to a point. But many people can tell you about God. Many religions.

What draws me to Jesus is that he lays aside his accreditation for the sake of others who need to discover God for themselves. Jesus won't spoon-feed his disciples. He refuses to make it all clear, all pretty and obvious, and tied up with a bow. "Who though he was in the form of God did not regard equality with God as something to be exploited" (Phil. 2:6). I take this to mean that Jesus refused to exploit his own divine connections because he knew it would get in the way of other people going to God. Jesus left us certain teachings as hints along the way. But he wasn't looking for passive listeners to those teachings who would "ooh" and "aah" over his "authorized" wisdom. Jesus, by emptying himself of credentials, invites others down the path to God. *By what authority are you doing these things, and who gave you this authority?* Jesus wouldn't say. And we ourselves cannot discover this authority until we start out down the path. Jesus wouldn't whip out his divine I.D. badge or provide the proper diploma and make it all clear. He wanted authentic followers—not admirers, not observers.

This discussion of Jesus' authority has important implications for the preacher's authority and the nature of sermons in a postmodern age where "truth" is perceived as relative and many skeptics doubt the possibility of an overarching "meta-narrative" like the Christian story "that gives focus, cohesion, commonality, and meaning to life."[4] Sermons that have a "Thus saith the Lord" feel to them simply will not work with this group (I will return to this point with the "seekers" group that follows).

What might begin to work with a skeptic (and my assumption throughout this book is that folk with a skeptical bent—many of whom are members—fill our pews every Sunday) is a playful cat and mouse approach where one's perceived authority is laid aside in favor of a mutual teasing out of the truth in sermonic form. There will be times when the preacher cannot compromise on a certain doctrinal stance (we shall discover this with the next sermon) but there is plenty of opportunity in many lectionary texts to take this open-ended approach in which the sermon is not jammed down the throat of a captive audience, fully explained and elucidated, but instead completed later on in the hearts and minds of the listeners. Katherine Paterson, author of the children's classic *Bridge to Terabithia*, makes an important point about parables that is equally valid for sermons delivered in a postmodern context:

> I have long been suspicious of the explanation of Jesus' parable of the sower. In his other parables, Jesus tells the story and leaves the learnings to his listeners. In the parable of the sower, in which, not

incidentally, an alert listener might find various meanings, Jesus, at the disciples' urging, spells out the intended message. Parables are literally "thrown beside." They leave the business of understanding to the audience. "He that has ears to hear, let him hear." I can't help but wonder if the explanation of the parable of the sower didn't have its seed in some first-century children's sermon.[5]

Sermons that playfully tease out the truth between the broad parameters of baptism and Eucharist (that is, within the meta-narrative) find their authority not in the preacher's credentials or perceived charisma, but to the extent that a listener is invited to take yet another step into the unknown with the crucified and risen Jesus. This is ultimately what forms a people capable of inviting "the poor, the crippled, the lame, and the blind" into table fellowship. Not a pastor's well-intentioned harangues. Nobel prize-winning author Anatole France (1844–1924) once said, "Do not try to satisfy your vanity by teaching a great many things. Awaken people's curiosity. It is enough to open minds; do not overload them. Put there just a spark. If there is some good flammable stuff, it will catch fire."[6]

At the end of this sermon I asked the fourteen skeptics to list two or three points from the sermon that stood out in their memories. One said, "It is good to share your hot beans and sauce, but it is easier for a rich man to pass through the eye of a needle than it is to get a child to share his cheese pizza." I'll accept that as an honest reflection of the truth.

CHAPTER THREE

Falling Short[1]

A Sermon for Reformation Sunday

*For there is no distinction, since all have sinned
and fall short of the glory of God; they are now justified by his grace as a gift. (Romans 3:22-24)*

I used to be an incredibly strict vegetarian and still
don't eat much meat except an occasional hot dog. A
good friend now calls me a "weenie vegetarian." But
there was a time when I scornfully and maybe judgmen-
tally avoided all flesh. It wasn't really for health reasons.
I just decided one day that I could no longer participate
in killing things and eating them for food. This went on
for a good ten years. The high moral road. The self-righ-
teous purist. I used to feign retching sounds into my
brothers' fishing bucket at the beach. Meatless propa-
ganda adorned our living room coffee table. My wife and
I even had a major tiff once in our little seminary apart-
ment because she'd chosen (horrors!) to make her brother a hamburger for supper. I saw this as caving in, major
sacrilege. Worth fighting for, truly.

Well, this went on for about a decade, living this pious
veggie righteousness, until one Thanksgiving several
years ago. We were in South Carolina with family there
and enjoyed the Thursday meal with all the trimmings. It
was all spread out before us and I, like the ten holidays
before this one, wordlessly bypassed the bird and dove
into the sweet potatoes. I ate my fill, audibly "gobbled" a
few times to poke fun, and we headed home.

It was a rainy and rather foggy return trip to Virginia.
Especially slow over the mountains. We rounded the cor-

ners cautiously, watching the guardrail, careful not to look down too long, entranced. Suddenly, appearing out of the fog, in full view in the lights, was a wild turkey that seemed to smile at me before I hit and killed it. My question: is there any greater irony for a pious vegetarian than to hit and kill the very bird he'd avoided at the dinner table for a decade?

A pastoral guess: all of us have probably rigged up pious improvement plans which show "that every day and in every way we are getting better and better." Perhaps we stand in judgment of the unenlightened who don't share our views. We believe that possible moral perfection might arrive if only we did this, avoided that, or spread the right information. Why, the kingdom might just come, if we got enough like-thinking people moving in the right direction. We could pull a whole world up by their moral bootstraps.

Basic Christian theology wants to especially say this: *we cannot save the world through proper moral behavior.* The world is not messed up due to ignorance or a simple lack of understanding. Christianity says the world is out of whack due to sin, a condition we're born with. In defining the word "sin," theologian Frederick Buechner says, "More even than hunger, poverty, or disease, it is what Jesus said he came to save the world from." Sin is not something we avoid—like meat at Thanksgiving—or a list of faults we've piously given up.

Several years ago, singer Johnny Cash appeared on a radio program in a southern city and he happened to mention a choice four-letter word during the interview. The next evening, a pastor appeared on the radio show and the phone lines lit up with calls about that word. One irate woman, a member of a local congregation, phoned in and said: "Pastor, what do you think of that awful word Johnny Cash used last night to pollute our airwaves?" The pastor replied, "What word, ma'am?" She said, "I'm a Christian, sir, and I don't say words like that." "Well," said the pastor, "*I* know a few bad words and I'll just say them one at a time. When I get to the word Johnny Cash used, you let me know. Okay?" The engineer had his finger close to the four-second delay button. "Let's see. Did Johnny Cash say the word *death*?" "No. That wasn't the word." "Okay, fine. I know others. Did he happen to say *nuclear war*?" "Well, no." "Let's try this one. How about *electric chair*?" By this time the woman had hung up, but the pastor couldn't resist: "Ma'am, I'm sorry you're not with us anymore. Hope you're listening at home. Those are three of the vilest, dirtiest words I know, and if Johnny Cash didn't say any of them and you won't tell me what he did say, then I guess I can't help you."[2]

So much of what transpires in the name of religion is actually an excuse for judging the behavior of others. It's easy to become the *Saturday Night Live* "Church Lady" doing our "superior dance." We are prone to self-righ-teousness and quick to look down our moral noses at those who make ethical goofs. Paul once wrote, and this is the great Reformation insight of Martin Luther: "For there is no distinction, since all have sinned and fall short of the glory of God." There's no distinction, he's saying. Whether you're the Archbishop of Canterbury or a resident on death row, *all* fall short. We disappoint people. We make the wrong decisions. We spend money foolishly. In Christian lingo, we sin. This is not something we acquire after a time of innocence. It's built in. Nor can we grow out of it.

This past week, someone was visiting our neighbor. We were all playing soccer out in the front yard, soaking up the incredible autumn sky. The visitor casually flicked a lit cigarette into the grass. Marta, who'd been up in a tree, waited for the man to go inside, and then called

Lukas over to see. She spoke softly, clinically, and with fascination: "You see this, Lukas? It's a *cigarette*." She almost whispered the word. "You don't ever want to start smoking these things. You can't quit and they might kill you." Lukas nodded gravely. "I know that," he said softly. They took turns stomping it out. But that wasn't the end of it. For the rest of the week, I noticed that they gave tours for other children over in the corner of the yard to see "the cigarette," which by now had become this fascinating symbol of what we should all avoid, but still holding an eerie power of attraction over them. Day after day, they went and searched for the very thing they'd been so effectively schooled to avoid.

Humanity's dance around the tree of the knowledge of good and evil begins early. We are powerfully drawn by the forbidden; that which has been deemed off-limits. So much of religion tries to form moral people by making sure we don't tiptoe past those limits and making sure we feel awful when we do. Our own Bible chronicles the folly of forming the godly by legislation. Read Deuteronomy closely sometime soon. And ditto with our own judicial system, come to think of it. Thirty years after the Civil Rights Act, Americans are still an incredibly bigoted people. Laws, religious or civil, will never change people's hearts. So what will?

In Christian theology, it took something drastic. It took a death—the death of Jesus, to be sure; for passion produces compassion, but centrally, the death of the law—the death of all our striving to be better and all of our guilt when we can't. Christ hangs there and says to his perpetrators, "Father, forgive them; for they do not know what they are doing" (Luke 23:34). One of the most shocking lines in all of scripture. God's judgment on humanity is this: "They are now justified by his grace as a gift" (Rom. 3:24). It's the truth, and it will set you free.

Somewhere up near Sam's Gap, the carcass of a dead turkey has long since rotted and returned to the soil—a turkey that smiled up in my headlights as I returned from Thanksgiving several years ago. I learned a lot from that turkey: that no one's hands are clean. Not one.

Sometimes when I think of that Thanksgiving, I think of Jesus hanging on the cross—the world's ultimate "turkey," so many said—now offered up for the feast. I think of all the ways I try to improve myself, justify myself in others' eyes. It doesn't work. Never has worked. And then I imagine him standing there in humanity's headlights. And do you know what? He is smiling, with arms open wide.

Response to the Sermon

Someone once asked Will Campbell, the salty, self-described "steeple dropout" from the Southern Baptist tradition, if he could define Christianity in ten words or less. Will scratched his chin and finally said, "We are all bastards, but God loves us anyway." That's nine words. He could have used just one: grace. The wonder of the Christian faith is found somewhere between the realization that God saved a wretch like *me*, but God also saves wretches like *them*. I'm not sure which is harder for us to accept.

In a world where we are getting better and smarter and savvier every day (or so we think), the notion of a Savior is downright repulsive to many. New Age thinking implies that I have all the spiritual resources I'll ever need, deep "within," and nothing outside the self is needed. *Voilà*. Homemade salvation. "Sin" in such a construct is only ecclesiastical baggage we carry from the past that can really be overcome with everything from t'ai chi to group therapy. Shopworn words like "confession" and "absolution" can only hinder the popular catechism that *I'm in control of my own destiny*. It's curious that Judy Collins' version of "Amazing Grace" has always been so popular with a "boomer" generation that is simultaneously repulsed by the theological notion of what this grace overcomes: sin.

On the other side of the spectrum are people of faith who cannot accept or believe that grace is actually extended to "miserable sinners" such as themselves. Deals are cut with God in my office. Penance for the past is real. Grace surely cannot be so simple as the father who races across the field, throws a robe and a ring on a lost son, and generally ignores the past. "Isn't there something I'm supposed to do to make amends? To earn God's favor? This is too simple. Aren't we in danger of making God the Ultimate Chump?"

Finally, grace oddly engenders not only humility and ceaseless striving in a congregation, but also downright anger. The prodigal's older brother lives. A congregation must regularly come to terms with its judgmental side and confess our commonality with "bad" people. The buzzword "inclusivity" truly begins here. What we have in common is sin and a Savior who gets a kick out of forgiving. Surprisingly, given the reactions below, one skeptic from the group agreed: "The realization that 'we are all sinners' is itself a great source of community and makes me realize that the difference between me and Jeffrey Dahmer is ontologically insignificant whatever my moral or ethical pretensions."

In writing and offering this sermon, I tried to keep in mind that God's grace doesn't always elicit hosannas in church and culture—disdain, disbelief, and disgust are also real reactions. All have honestly been part of my own spiritual topography down through the years. I *believe* baptism to be grace in liquid form. I'm a Lutheran, for crying out loud! But, I still get sucked into all the cozy deals with the law and works righteousness. The old Adam is still a good swimmer, even though we claim to drown him at font's edge.

I suppose I've known much of this for some time, but one discovery that surprised me a bit in my work with skeptics was an almost across-the-board resistance to the concept of unconditional grace. The Lutheran trump card! Our ace in the hole! The group found the ethical/ social Jesus admirable and commendable. They did not feel the same about the Jesus who comes to save us from sin. "I suppose your sermon is supposed to lead one to conclude that while our moral behavior can't save the world, Jesus' coming to rid the world of sin can. If this is what you meant to convey, I have no idea what it means . . . to a nonbeliever, this sermon was filled with sentences that make no sense to me, and ideas with which I disagree." Only three of the fourteen participants reacted favorably to this Reformation Sunday sermon based on a traditional doctrine at the heart of the faith.

This second sermon was where people really began to share where they differed with basic Christian theology. "I was not expecting to be so irritated by the concept of original sin as I was. This is a main problem for me with religion. I prefer to think of all people as basically good but prone to make the wrong choices sometimes based on various influences." Another admitted: "It's that word 'sin' that sticks in my craw. Whenever I hear it, I think of a painting from the Middle Ages depicting the earth and all its inhabitants being excreted out of the anus of Satan." "The whole concept of 'Jesus died for my sins' is ridiculous to me," said yet another terse and honest respondent.

When asked to define the word "grace," most wrote that the word did not function in their everyday lives and the concept made little sense. Resistance to the idea fell into several categories. First, because many did not accept the idea that all people have "sinned," they concluded that some people would not require grace to address that sin. Second, several felt that radical grace and unconditional acceptance let obvious tyrants "off the hook" too easily. (I found this point to be a bit ironic; several of the participants found it important to judge wrongdoings of others, but not to acknowledge their own complicity in the evils of the world nor to accept the traditional name for that involvement.) Third, some noted that if God makes no distinctions between people, that we have "all sinned and fallen short," then what's the point of the moral life? One put it this way: "The sermon could be used as a justification for not taking moral stands. Grace promotes a fatalism that I have heard used time and again to justify inaction in the face of injustice. This type of theology is one of the reasons I am not comfortable attending church." Similarly: "To depend on grace allows you to relax, but it also takes the challenge of acting out a 'good life' away." Finally, their responses suggest that belief in no God eventually forces a person to credit "chance" rather than grace when pressed to explain life's unmerited gifts. "If God gives us grace, where is he so much of the time?"

I was honestly not prepared for such a variety of responses. As a Lutheran, I've always assumed that our focus on grace and God's benevolent gifts was naturally appealing to a culture drowning in a sea of law. I discovered exactly the opposite with this test group. Not only was grace a foreign idea in their lives, it generally made them angry to hear it preached so baldly. Theologian Ted Peters offers a helpful insight here:

> Inherent in sin is the denial of truth. We cover our unwholesome motives and violent acts against others with a veneer of goodness. We sugarcoat our

garbage. Everyone has a stake in hiding the truth of sin. This makes uncovering the mystery of how sin works difficult, because wherever we dig, lies rush in to fill the hole. Perhaps an objective or scholarly approach to the truth of sin is foredoomed from the start. Perhaps the only way to get at the truth of sin is through confession.[3]

Millard Fuller of Habitat for Humanity tells a story that illustrates this truth quite well. Several years ago I heard Millard address the National Press Club on public radio and he recalled a workshop at Pittsburgh Theological Seminary with two hundred pastors in attendance. The assembled pastors quickly pointed toward greed and selfishness as reasons the church never had enough money to assist others creatively. Millard then asked this seemingly innocent question: "Is it possible for a person to build a house so large that it's sinful in the eyes of God? Raise your hand if you think so." All two hundred pastors raised their hands. "Okay," said Millard, "then can you tell me at exactly what *size*, the precise square footage, a certain house becomes sinful to occupy?" Silence from the pastors. You could have heard a pin drop. Finally a small, quiet voice spoke up from the back of the room: "When it's bigger than mine." I think it's somehow appropriate that this story is told on preachers who may be so busy pointing out sin in others that they miss it in themselves. "Perhaps the only way to get at the truth of sin," says Peters, "is through confession." Ditto for the pulpit—perhaps especially for the pulpit.

Christians profess that God's dealing gracefully with the sin and evil in each of us is likely to evoke gratitude from us. In the future when I preach on this I will focus more on the personal change and transformation birthed by God's grace. It's easy to get stuck in a doctrinal defense of how it all works. Perhaps the greatest heresy of our age is that we still believe we can save ourselves and this world with a little more moral elbow grease. The images used in the sermon (a dead turkey, a judgmental woman, and a child fascinated with the forbidden) were specific and concrete enough to reveal the insidious nature of our sin. But sermons in this area also need to show concretely *how* grace makes a difference in a particular life. I perhaps spent too much time dabbling in the limits of self-improvement.

This may be a good place to mention a couple of homiletical revelations that occurred midway through my time with this group. My original goal was to preach a "regular" Sunday sermon and try to forget the test group was even present, having them "overhear" and then respond. I found this to be impossible. Preaching persuades. It isn't possible to preach in a vacuum with others "watching" you from a coldly analytical and scientific viewpoint.

Second, I suddenly realized that people like those in my test group were walking into worship practically every week. To preach with only the congregation of parish members in mind seemed to be a rather narrow understanding of the Holy Spirit who is constantly stirring the hearts and minds of newcomers to appear at worship—when? The preacher should assume it's this Sunday, every Sunday. Jack Miles writes: "Americans have not so much recovered their faith in religion as lost their faith in the alternatives. . . . Though many people who turn up in church and synagogue are not truly believers, they are not hypocrites either. What appeals to them in the first instance may be the social and esthetic refuge provided by religion, but they arrive with open minds regarding belief."[4] My homiletics shifted to include "skeptics" as part of my permanent sermonic planning. There is more doubt in the pews each week than most pastors imagine.

This new understanding suggests that preachers must be careful in assuming that old words like "sin," "grace," and "redemption" are immediately and universally understood by a secular culture. One popular tack to attract postmodern worshipers is to edit all such "final" language out of our Sunday morning vocabularies. Scott Cairns, of the Orthodox tradition, offers his playful poem dripping with irony:

> I suppose we might do away with words like *sin*.
> They are at least archaic, not to mention rude,
> and late generations have been pretty well schooled
>
> against the presumption of holding *anything*
> to be absolutely so, universally
> applicable, especially anything like
>
> *sin* which is, to put it more neatly, unpleasant,
> not the sort of thing one brings up . . .[5]

Cairns would argue that "bringing up" such timeless theological conundrums that describe the human condition is exactly what preachers, albeit confessionally, are called to do. There is much at stake here. "Churches have so often turned the word 'sin' into an instrument of oppression and an assault on sexuality that it's hard to come by its meaning honestly."[6] True enough. But ridding our vocabulary of the word is hardly the answer. I recall viewing novelist Mary Gordon on the Bill Moyers' *Genesis* special on PBS several years ago. There were several New Age types on the show, and after listening to panelists politely tiptoe around the issue Gordon finally blurted out, "People just aren't *right*. There is something fundamentally *wrong* with us that we cannot fix ourselves."

Excising offensive theological vocabulary in the name of inclusion is usually a mistake. In the case of the word "sin," such an attempt often encourages several things. It means we are forever blaming others for our problems. We fail to see ourselves as we truly are. We are blocked from the wonderful liberation of confession and forgiveness. And we fail to tap into the grace that can truly heal us. One recent returnee to church life in our parish confided to me not long ago how the "confession of sin" in the liturgy was the most important part of the service for him. The reason we baptize babies, after all, in our tradition is not that they're sweet; not that Jesus loved children; and not because it's a swell thing to include them. All of those things are true, of course. But we baptize babies because it's *appropriate*. It's appropriate because we believe sin is not something one grows into but rather something that's built-in and comes with the territory. "Sin, it seemed to Augustine, is a hereditary disease. We are in want of a cure."[7] Sermons need *more* nuanced theological depth, not less (a "Sermon Lite" in order to appeal to the masses). But, the poet and my skeptics have a point. Traditional language is often lost on the secular ear. "The problem," says Barbara Brown Taylor, "is not so much that the words have been kidnapped by a hostile gang, who have used them so roughly that their meaning has been bruised. Instead, the problem is that they sound like words from another age, as outdated to many ears as 'beseech' and 'vouchsafe.' "[8]

What do we mean by "original sin"? How do we paint fresh pictures of "God's grace" in a judgmental world? What does "redemption" mean for someone living in the twenty-first century? I think of a scene from the movie *Saving Private Ryan* where Captain John Miller, played by Tom Hanks, finally locates Private James Francis Ryan behind enemy lines in order to tell him that his three brothers, all soldiers, are dead. Some time after receiving this news, Private Ryan (Matt Damon) says, "I can't see my brothers' faces. I've been trying and I can't see their faces at all. Does that ever happen to you?" "You've got to think of a context," says Captain Miller. "What does that mean?" Private Ryan asks. "You just don't think about their faces. You think of something specific, something you've done together. When I want to think of home I think of my old hammock, my wife pruning rose bushes, a pair of my old work gloves."[9] Preaching in a postmodern era will require a specific, vivid context in order to enliven old, important words. Preaching will require something of the poet's eye, "imaginative speech that permits people to enter into new worlds of faith and to participate in joyous, obedient life."[10]

I was heading down Main Street one afternoon not long ago, approaching our church near the railroad overpass, and heard an odd scraping sound that traveled down the entire length of my Subaru roof. "Oh *no*," I thought. Or maybe I said some other word. It was that sinking, helpless feeling of knowing you've left something on the top of your car, utterly powerless now to do anything about it. You are at the mercy of gravity and wind. You cringe and wince.

I glanced in the rearview mirror just in time to see a videotape rented from Al's Video II bounce several times along the pavement. It was bouncing like a ball right down the center line of Highway 11, bouncing until finally the plastic jacket separated from the naked tape, like a banana from its peel. One landed off the road on the shoulder and the other finally came to rest in the middle of my lane. I could not tell which was which from the distance that now separated us. I did, however, know the approximate market value of a "new release." So, after watching all of this painfully in the mirror, I whipped off the road, threw open the door, and started running. The lane was clear. Maybe I could still rescue it.

The driver of the truck that topped the bridge must have wondered why a man in street shoes and dress clothes was running toward him at such a frenzied speed. It was a valiant try, but there was no way to reach it in time. I was about to witness a celluloid death.

As I ran, the excuses, the avoidance, the downright fabrications started to form in my mind. How could I get out of this? What story could I make up as I gingerly placed the mangled movie on the return desk? Maybe I could use the night deposit at Al's and they wouldn't notice. Maybe I could make it look like it was somehow *their* fault. Maybe I could righteously report that this was a bad movie, a *very bad* movie, and I as a minister of God was protecting other local citizens from its inherent moral repulsion. As I ran, there was something dark and primitive and sinister already luring me to lie about this. To somehow escape blame. To avoid responsibility. It was a voice, a strong, audible voice.

I don't know what you'd call it. I'd call it sin—hardly original, but a part of me that I can't fix by myself. That'll preach in any century, any culture.

CHAPTER FOUR

Raising Hell or Lowering Heaven?

A Sermon for the Second Sunday of Advent

In those days John the Baptist appeared in the wilderness of Judea, proclaiming,"Repent, for the kingdom of heaven has come near." (Matthew 3:1-2)

In those days. In *these* days "John the Therapist" appears in the foothills of the Poconos and purrs, "Chill out. I'm okay and you're okay. Slip into the jacuzzi here and be baptized in the name of all that feels good and is intellectually relevant. Be embraced by the warm-fuzzy lingo of luuuv, unconditional acceptance, and world peace without sacrifice. The problems you're having aren't your fault. Goodness no. You're just a victim. A victim of your past. We all are! There's nothing wrong with you that a little massage therapy won't fix. So come on in. Light the gas logs and feel the cozy fire. Have a glass of wine. Chill out! In the name of the Karma, and of the Irresponsible Fun, and of the Wholly In Touch With My Inner Child. Amen."

"Repent," says John the Baptist. The word literally means, "turn." Go in another direction. Take a 180-degree ongoing detour toward God. In an era where we have largely abandoned a vocabulary of sin and redemption to describe our predicament and need, John the Baptist is almost too much. His words in the wilderness today make Billy Graham sound like Mr. Rogers. Listen again to this assortment of images: camel's hair, locusts, snakes, fire, and an ax. Aren't these nice Merry Christmas images, boys and girls?

Believe it or not, I own a *camel's hair* athletic supporter (yes, I do) given to me last year by a friend in this congregation who will go unnamed (oh, what the heck—it was Barry Proctor).* And when the seventeen-year *locusts* came out in Frederick County when we lived there, the local 4-H Center claimed those loud insects were exceptionally high in protein, so they published recipes. Yes. An apple farmer in our church ate a few, so I guessed I could, too. *Snakes* don't bother me much. My brother used to keep a brood until they somehow escaped into the den one night. We never found them. My mother banned serpents in the house after that. And here's an *ax*, if any of you people get out of line and stop bearing fruit. So, maybe I could be John the Baptist with some practice. Give me a month in the Mount Rogers wilderness to work on an attitude and come on up.

But it's John's image of Jesus as a fire-bringer (isn't it?) that troubles so many modern Christians. "He will baptize you with the Holy Spirit and fire . . . he will gather wheat . . . but the chaff he will burn with unquenchable fire" (Matt. 3:11-12). It's a bit more graphic than gas logs, I'll admit. Unquenchable. The New Testament Greek word here is *asbestos*. Just like the stuff that won't burn that colleges now rip out of dormitory ceilings because it's a carcinogen. The image is of a fire that won't be burned up. Which is also a common image of hell, of course. Is that John's main message—hell? The wheat represents good people and the chaff bad, right? Maybe not. Because wheat and chaff are part of the same kernel of grain, perhaps John is describing what the Coming One will do in the life of an individual person, the same person. His winnowing fork is in his hand. One who is baptized into the Coming One's kingdom is repeatedly tossed into the winds of the Holy Spirit until the chaff

---

*Used with Barry Proctor's permission.

and the hulls are blown out of our lives—an ongoing process. Jesus came to help us become fruit for others, and to burn up all that stands in his way.

What John is describing here today is conversion— submission to an unrelenting power and force that will not leave us alone until we glow with a fire that is God. John's words today are not so much a threat as a promise. A promise that God's spirit will go to extraordinary measures to blow the chaff out of our lives. We resist this on a number of levels. First, because such an image of Jesus doesn't square with an adoration of America's favorite baby whom we drape with tinsel and serenade with mall music this time of year. How can that baby bring fire into my life? He's too cute! We're disturbing the Gospel According to Norman Rockwell. Second, we resist such a picture of Jesus because deep down many of us believe we need no help beyond ourselves. We pride ourselves in being self-sufficient. We don't need a Savior. We only need an affirmed image of the ego. Turn on the gas logs and create a mood. That's the most fire many ever need. We give up on the holy fire of God because we see such as pure threat rather than promise.

Jesus doesn't save us *from* something, such as hell. But rather *for* something: to bear good fruit. Historically, the saints who lived most radically for others were in touch with a power far greater than the self, a power that transformed them into totally different people—a fire that almost obliterated the self until they lived wholly for God. Aflame.

In one of C. S. Lewis's stories about Narnia, *The Voyage of the Dawn Treader*, a little boy named Eustace is so self-absorbed that he finally turns into a dragon—the outward embodiment of what he had become on the inside. Just when it seems that Eustace will have to be left behind (because a dragon wouldn't fit on the ship in which Eustace and his friends were traveling) Aslan the Lion (the Christ figure in the stories) appears and leads him to a well. "I knew it was a well," Eustace later reports, "because you could see the water bubbling up from the bottom of it: but it was a lot bigger than most wells—like a very big, round bath with marble steps going down into it. The lion told me I must undress first." So Eustace tries. But as soon as one layer of dragon skin is peeled off, another grows back just as fast. Three times a scaly suit of skin is peeled off and three times it grows back. Eustace thinks to himself: "Oh dear, how ever many skins have I got to take off? . . . Then the lion said, 'You will have to let me undress you.' The very first tear was so deep that I thought it had gone right into my heart. And when he began pulling the skin off, it hurt worse than anything I've ever felt. Then he caught hold of me and threw me into the water. It smarted like anything, but only for a moment. After that it became perfectly delicious, and then I saw why. I'd turned into a boy again. After a bit the lion took me out and dressed me."[1]

In *The Seven Storey Mountain*, Thomas Merton calls his baptism, "My happy execution and rebirth. What mountains were falling off my shoulders! What scales of dark night were peeling off my intellect to let in the inward vision of God and his truth. Christ born in me, a new Bethlehem, and sacrificed in me, his new Calvary, and risen in me."[2]

Eustace the former dragon and Thomas Merton have much in common. They finally discovered who must undress them and who must truly serve as midwife in their rebirth. Sometimes painfully, we turn toward a God who won't leave us just as we are.

John the Baptist was on fire for God. Maybe he offended some. Diogenes, the Greek philosopher who lived three centuries before Jesus, once said: "He who never offended anyone, never did anyone any good." Someone has suggested, though, that the sign of a real prophet is not that they raise hell, but that they lower heaven. I like that. And, I think John the Baptist did that very thing.

"Repent," said the man from the wilderness. Turn. Why? Because you'll burn forever if you don't? No. "Because the kingdom of heaven has come near." Closer than we know. And Christ has chaff to blow out of your life that you alone cannot remove.

Thursday. That somewhat unexpected blanket of snow that so beautifully covered everything last Thursday morning hid the imperfections of our lives and the ugly places in our little town. It was so quiet. We need such breaks, when we can bundle down in the bed and hide. Pretending as if the world's problems and ours don't exist. Under the covers.

Conversely, Jesus is the One who uncovers. He reveals our idols and securities and asks us to surrender them. He exposes the chaff of our lives and promises to slowly burn it away. He throws us in the water until we are wholly and completely his.

We are not scared into change by threats or a well-intentioned prophet raising hell out in the woods. In Christ, God has lowered heaven—the kingdom has come near with his birth in the world. In those days. And in you, in these.

Response to the Sermon

There is a wonderful story told about the great sculptor Michelangelo. Neighbors once saw him pushing a huge piece of rock down a street in his native Florence. One of the neighbors, sitting on her front porch, shook her head in amazement and called out to him: "I always knew the Buonarrotis were crazy. Why do you bother over that old piece of stone?" To which the great artist replied: "Because there is an angel in that rock that wants to come out." That's not a bad way to look at Advent. God sees more in us than we sometimes see. God takes the raw materials of our lives and shapes and tinkers and dreams and sculpts with the chisel of his Word until a whole new person is born—converted, to use the old word. We are works of art in process.

We who take our Christmas with lots of sugar don't cozy up to John's fire this time of year. He demands repentance, conversion, good fruit, and change from each of the dipped. He challenges both ritual ("Who warned you to show up?") and lineage ("Just because your daddy's name is on every commemorative plaque in the building doesn't mean you're right with God"), two of the most cherished bastions of any congregation. John would agree with those who claim that God has no grandchildren. Each generation of would-be Christians must come to terms with Jesus through a death and rebirth. William Willimon has written: "When you join the Rotary they give you a handshake and a lapel pin. When you join the church we throw you in the water and half drown you. Ponder that. Whatever signing on with Jesus means, it means that we will not do just as we are, that change is demanded, daily, sometimes painful turning and detoxification that does not come naturally."[3]

In large part, most mainline churches leave John the Baptist for the fundamentalists or the street-corner preachers who rail fire and brimstone. "Conversion" is for the weepy or the weak and "repentance" is just a psychological downer in a world with enough bad news already. We *enlightened* Protestants know what we're not, but sometimes have a devil of a time explaining who we are. Maybe it's time for the church to take a fresh look at this wild one of the wilderness and the new life toward which he points in this or any season.

One of the questions I was trying to raise in this sermon was: "How do people change?" The opening vignette was a playful attempt to expose our cultural reliance on a variety of tools for transformation other than God. Many baby boomers are very thirsty for change in their lives and truly sense something is wrong, but do not want to be confronted with their own complicity (sin) in terms of what ails them. We usually opt for a variety of psychological tonics, pop therapies and fad feel-good exercises that do little to affect true, ongoing rebirth. Robert Coles, himself a renowned psychologist, writes:

> Why is it that psychiatry now has so much intellectual, and yes, moral authority among the clergy? . . . I wonder whether the deepest mire . . . may be found in the dreary solipsistic world so many of us have learned to find so interesting: the mind's moods, the various "stages" and "phases" of "human development" or of "dying," all dwelt upon (God save us!) as if Stations of the Cross.[4]

I continued to learn from the responses of my test group. In many ways, a person like John the Baptist (an obvious hell-raiser) appealed to many of the folk in this group who are fairly liberal and interested in social change. A continued cutting edge in our differences was how this social change might come about. Ultimately, Christians change because they sense the kingdom of God has come near. We are transformed because we assent to a Christ who is drawing our lives more and more into concert with his own. Because we live in an age where the predominant understanding of change comes from "within" a storehouse of personal resources, not from divine, outside help, I did not expect my group of skeptics to like this sermon.

"For me, transformation has almost always occurred in a moment. I just mentally change—a conscious act." "When I focus on the realities of what is happening in my community and what I might be able to do about it, it's not because I have a desire to please Jesus or God. I just know it is the right thing to do." (I desperately wanted to ask how the respondent believes one comes to know this.) A third participant noted: "You seem to say we are pissants if we think we don't need a savior and can change ourselves. . . . It seems to me that hinting that a savior is necessary to guide one through change is a knock, however unintended, on many religions of the world. There are legitimate alternatives to those you present." This last point was echoed by one who said, "We need spiritual help to undertake this task [of repentance] but I find it distracting and limiting to call that help 'Jesus' . . . too much focus is forced into the energy of being 'Lutheran' or 'Protestant' or 'Christian' or even 'Islamic.' A final person admitted that it was "hard to tell the difference between most people before and after the conversion experience.'" "It bothers me that modern Christianity still places a premium on what you 'believe' as opposed to how you act."

Many people in the group suggested that change for them usually occurs "through an extreme occurrence like a life-threatening experience or the death of one's close relatives or friends," a general awareness of the shortness of life and our common mortality. Although a frustrating commentary on our culture for preachers interested in social change and transformation, such popular sentiment is also an accurate assessment of why most people consider taking a different direction with their lives—a crisis occurs, death stares one in the face.

... And then one day the doorbell rang. A salesman said, *Watch this!* He stripped my bed and vacuumed it. The nozzle sucked up two full, measured cups of light gray flakes. He said, *That's human skin.* I stood, refusing the purchase, stood staring at her flesh and mine commingled inside the measuring cup, stood there and thought, *She's been gone two years, she's married, and all this time her flesh has been in bed with me. Don't laugh. Don't laugh.*[5]

Reflection upon one's mortality is a powerful impetus for change. Many mentioned this as a factor in their lives. In fairness, one also noted "extraordinary kindness" and "witnessing the courageous acts of others, especially those you know" as dual inspiration for personal change.

This sermon touched a sensitive nerve. Although most did not agree with the method presented (the "undressing" of the obnoxious Eustace the dragon and his subsequent "baptism"), all wrote thoughtfully about the need for change in their own lives and how that occurs for them. In their defense, they were also particularly open to the charges that, as one put it: "Our culture places far too much emphasis on individual self-sufficiency."

I found it necessary to deal head on with various images of fire and judgment raised in the lectionary text. So many church dropouts recall images of fear and damnation as dominant memories from childhood. Lingering questions of how a good God can threaten eternal punishment to bring about loving behavior are still very real for many survivors of rigid fundamentalism. Several found it helpful to discover that John's use of the word "fire" is not necessarily the fire of condemnation, but perhaps the fire (Greek = *pur*) that purifies, converts, and empowers (such as the fire of Pentecost). "I like the idea of getting rid of the 'chaff' in ourselves much better than burning sinners in hellfire." The challenge of this sermon was confronting traditional notions of hell and judgment without taking the edge off John's prophetic urgency. I wanted to be clear on how and why true change comes about from a Christian perspective—not through fear; not through willpower or intellect alone (illustrations of Eustace and Merton); not primarily through "raising hell" with the powers that be—but rather through submitting to Christ who reveals our foibles, blows the chaff out of our lives, and allows us to bear fruit. Ultimately, Christians change because they sense the kingdom of God has come near. True discipleship is more of a pull than a push.

To reach people in this area with future sermons, it might be wise to acknowledge the true, ongoing struggle for change that is already happening in people's lives. I fear I made light of that too much. "[You were] somewhat dismissive of the painful, difficult work therapy is for most people." Probably true. My test group wanted to change—that's more than I can say of many Christians. They simply saw a rather narrow, internal field of resources to assist them. That popular construct was very much in mind as I wrote this sermon and thought about my listeners.

As I read the responses to this sermon from these fourteen skeptics, I was reminded again of the precarious position of a sinful, glaringly inadequate pastor like me, with myriad shortcomings, who calls a congregation to holiness and change. One skeptic beautifully exposed this difficulty in all who work for change by admitting: "A call to repentance lays out for people our favorite idols, helps us to experience the fakery, and rejoices in our lucky release from them. I'm afraid I would need a lot more camel hair and locusts to get away with calling people to repentance and, even then, the best I could hope for is my head on a platter." I recall a visit to Lake

Winnepesaukah, an amusement park near my parents' home in Chattanooga, Tennessee. There is a Sky Buckets ride there that lifts the amused over Lake Winnie and back. As you head across the water, pairs of people are returning. You pass quite closely, wave, and never see them again in this life. On our trip across the lake, my brother and I noticed a young boy heading toward us. He could not have been more than twelve and was just lighting up a cigarette. High above the water, I smiled and said this as we passed: "Those things will kill you, young man." He looked at me, perplexed, and we passed out of each other's lives forever.

What came over me? What business is this of mine, really? Indeed, could this advice not have been construed as rude? The prevailing wisdom in our country of independence and freedom is that we leave each other alone in the name of tolerance and acceptance, especially if that behavior "isn't hurting anyone." Even when the behavior seems clearly detrimental, it is still very difficult to confront a friend with the truth. There is a precariousbalancing act between "speaking the truth in love" (Eph. 4:15) and appearing judgmental and holier-than-thou. Many of the skeptics in my test group grew up in churches where the preacher tried to scold them into righteousness. Pastors need to be very careful that the pulpit does not begin to resemble a "Sky Bucket" aiming well-intentioned advice at people from a safe distance. Part of this means being especially open to revealing our own shortcomings and struggles, confessing from the pulpit our mutual sinfulness in matters of faithfulness (see especially Jesus' advice about the log and speck in Matt. 7:1-5). We hold each other accountable, ultimately, not to self-righteously point fingers, but in order that members of a Christian community "grow up in every way into him" (the second half of Ephesians

4:15). Preaching repentance is difficult, agonizing work, approached with holy humility.

Finally, I need to confess that this sermon began to raise my frustration level with my own project ground rules. I promised from the onset that no one from the church (including me) would contact anyone in any way. But the responses of the group, though well written in most cases, were limiting in their lack of dialogue. I was not able to acknowledge responses either of an insightful or ridiculous nature. This was difficult and eventually affected the way I normally preach, in that I tried to cram too much material into a single sermon, perhaps trying to say everything I could about Christianity while I had them around. Kenneth Untener offers practical advice for preachers who might get carried away with the role of the sermon in the wider scheme of the liturgy: "When it comes to homilies (especially homilies for major events) we tend to imagine something large. Homilies are important, but they aren't large: They're a small part of this large, grand event called the liturgy. When I think of homilies as something small, everything changes. I search for the pearl of great price. A pearl is something worth listening to."[6] In retrospect, this underscores a conviction learned from our catechumenal ministry: conversion is not a moment in time, but a lengthy initiation into a tradition that unfolds over many years and many conversations.[7] These skeptics helped me remember that again.

CHAPTER FIVE

Following a Stranger

A Sermon for the
Third Sunday After the Epiphany

Jesus left Nazareth and made his home in Capernaum by the sea. (Matthew 4:13)

When Jesus was about thirty years old, or maybe in his late twenties, he left home for good. Presumably, he said good-bye to his parents and headed for the sea. Nazareth, his hometown, was in the mountains and he walked northeast toward water, losing elevation as he traveled. He eventually came to a place called Capernaum, a bustling fishing village on the northern edge of the sea, only about twenty-five miles from home as the crow flies, but a world away from his roots. It is here that our story says he "made his home," using the town as a central base of sorts. He made a special return trip there once to heal Peter's mother-in-law. It was here that he healed a paralytic man whose friends lowered him through the roof of the house where Jesus was. And, it was just off the coast of Capernaum that Jesus walked on water; fairly nearby that he fed five-thousand. He would return here several times throughout his ministry.

Capernaum became the base of his kingdom operations. It gave him quick access to major transportation routes, and it was a gateway of sorts to non-Jewish, Gentile territories, a foreshadowing of the light his life would become for all people who once sat in darkness and the shadow of death.

But here's what I don't get. This is what continually

amazes me about this story: when Jesus moved to Capernaum, he knew nobody. If he had relatives in town, we aren't told. No bodacious miracles were pulled off following or preceding his arrival. Not yet. In short, he had no reputation when he walked into that town. *Nobody* knew him from Adam. Now maybe he checked into a little bed and breakfast there and the proprietor found him kind of special. Maybe he watched the boats come in for a few days down at the docks and got a feel for the county economy. Maybe he ate at the local fish and chips joint and got the local lowdown from Babs the waitress. Maybe it got around that some guy who knew the Torah pretty well lived downtown.

But, even if all of that happened, we still aren't prepared for two sets of brothers leaving their jobs and family in the middle of some fine afternoon to go off and follow a stranger! For that's the bald truth of it. Peter, Andrew, James and John drop everything and follow some guy they've never seen or spoken to. "Follow me, and I will make you fish for people." And then—boom—without a break in the text: "Immediately they left their nets and followed." Not the next day. Not when they could clock out from work. Not when they could make sure daddy Zebedee was happy. Then. They got up and went. Went right after somebody who five minutes before didn't exist for them. Can you imagine this?

Frankly, I can't. We have a hard enough time following Jesus in our own lives with the benefit of Bibles. We can even tune in to somebody saying something about Jesus twenty-four hours a day. This country is saturated with words and religious trinkets about the man. Every aspect of his person has been microscopically examined by scholars, and yet even now, with all our information and insight, it's those two little words, "Follow me," that trip us up and leave us reaching for excuses, rationalizations, and explanations that he couldn't have possibly meant that. Given our latter-day disobedience to the invitation, can you imagine how in the world these first four disciples left everything to follow a stranger? Forgive me, but I can't! This story has my vote for the most radical and disturbing in the Gospels.

Romulus Linney, a playwright, in his book titled *Jesus Tales*, has gathered a number of humorous, apocryphal stories about our Lord that are told around the world but won't appear in any Bible. One of the stories, from Hungary, is told from the perspective of Peter's wife (he was presumably married if he had a mother-in-law). She is getting rather tired of Peter leaving all the time and running off on trips with Jesus, never home with the children. "He's a fraud," she says, "you poor fool." Peter gets a faraway twinkle in his eye. "He's a God," is the answer he confidently offers. Put out with this foolishness and not convinced, his wife says tersely, "My foot."[1]

And that's where most sane people, including most Christians, draw the line with Jesus. For you see, no matter what the political Religious Right wants to say about our Lord, he's not really the best guy to promote our country's current understanding of traditional "family values." In fact, the way I read Jesus, he's constantly breaking up the notion of Mom, Dad, 2.2 kids, a doghouse, and a chain-link fence in the backyard, and inviting us into a new family, the family of God. The mention of James and John "leaving their father" in the boat to follow Jesus is a clear message to all who might come after. We are called to leave home and find a true home with Jesus. That is a central point of this story.

But, maybe not the main point. This story is not so much about leaving as it is about following—putting our whole life and our ultimate trust and security in the one we call Jesus. That's a fearful thing to do for most of us.

It is fearful, ultimately, not because of the demands Jesus might place on our family and our vocation, which are admittedly imposing, but because Jesus is still so much a stranger to us. Even though those first four disciples followed Jesus without knowing who he was, we have a hard time doing so. We moderns have so many questions we need answered about anybody or anything before we can throw our trust and commitment into the ring. We are naturally suspicious about universal claims. Peter, Andrew, James and John got up and without a word followed someone who spoke and lived with authority. Today we would never do such a thing. Most feel a need to have everything worked out about every facet of Christian doctrine ranging from original sin to the resurrection of the body before entertaining even a remote possibility of following Jesus. This is not to say that questions and intellectual inquiry are unimportant. It is to say that this first story of discipleship underscores obedience prior to enlightenment. The first disciples began their journey before they fully knew who Jesus was. And maybe it was only in following Jesus that they would *ever* find out.

Could the same be true today? Are we moderns waiting until we're fully convinced, until we have enough information, until somebody can prove it beyond the shadow of a doubt before we follow Jesus? Well, what if that's not the way one discovers the real truth of the man? What if insight is only possible precisely through obedient following, as this story suggests? It's interesting to me that Jesus never says, "Well, hi, I'm Jesus of Nazareth and I have a set of theological principles I'd like for you to consider before joining me." Or, "Work out in your own mind your beliefs about God and I'll come back tomorrow and check if they square with mine." No. Jesus doesn't invite us to have it all worked out before we begin. This stranger says, "Follow me." And *in the going* is insight.

I am convinced that it's impossible to eternally "study" Jesus with any real depth of lasting insight. I'm also convinced that it's impossible to "understand" Jesus just by talking about him or just by becoming a member of a church. Here's what I think. Jesus is fully revealed to his disciples, slowly and in layers, only when we take the first tentative steps of following in his way and living his life. Not before. Without this obedience and trust, without this attempt to bring our lives into concert with his, Jesus is indecipherable and we are only playing at church. We will be sidetracked time and again by interesting questions that entertain our intellects, but can't touch our hearts. "Follow me," he says. Notice that he doesn't say, "Admire me" or "Believe in me" or "Make sure you've got every single line of the Apostles' Creed worked out first." No. Follow me. It's a lot like falling in love. The insights you glean about your beloved cannot be totally worked out and discovered before the commitment occurs. They are revealed, these insights, as the relationship matures.

Shel Silverstein, the late poet and artist, has a great poem that captures something of the terror, the strangeness, and the promise of today's story at Capernaum. The poem is titled "The One Who Stayed."

> You should have heard the old men cry
> You should have heard the biddies
> When that sad stranger raised his flute
> And piped away the kiddies.
> Katy, Tommy, Meg and Bob
> Followed, skipping gaily,
> Red-haired Ruth, my brother Rob,
> And little crippled Bailey,
> John and Nils and Cousin Claire,
> Dancin', spinnin', turnin'

'Cross the hills to God knows where—
They never came returnin'.
'Cross the hills to God knows where
The piper pranced, a leadin'
Each child in Hamlin Town but me
And I stayed home unheedin'.
My papa says that I was blest
For if that music found me,
I'd be witch-cast like all the rest.
This town grows old around me.
I cannot say I did not hear
That sound so haunting hollow—
I heard, I heard, I heard it clear . . .
I was afraid to follow.[2]

Response to the Sermon

I have a cartoon titled "Global Village Idiot" tacked to my office door depicting a manic computer nut parked in front of his screen. He's yelling: "Go ahead, ask me any question! Anything! I'm linked to every bulletin board and information network on the planet! I'll have an answer in seconds. 'Course, I won't be able to put it into any meaningful context, but who needs that?"

Awash in information for information's sake, American culture is less and less intrigued by mystery and uncertainty. We like verifiable data and scientific surety. Hard facts. Our favorite national posture is one of arms folded tightly across a chest challenging, "Prove it. Convince me."

This has vast implications for the church. What is the relationship between science and faith? How do congregations invite potential adult converts into a living relationship with Jesus when those same adults come from jobs and worlds that encourage (nay, require) hard evidence or a reasonable hunch based on previous truths before proceeding? Let's admit it. Our nation worships

the intellect, the rational response. In one of his monologues about a boy he grew up with, Garrison Keillor
reflects on why so many are typically uneasy around
mentally challenged people: "We feel that intelligence is
the fundamental part of being human; that our minds,
what we think and what we imagine—that's us, our
minds. At least that's what we think. And so when
we see these injured people, we feel pity for them and
we feel uneasy around them."[3] A history of institution-
alization and wholesale hiding of the mentally ill in this
country is also a facet of this uneasiness. Dan Quayle
misquoted the motto of the American Negro College
Fund ("A mind is a terrible thing to waste") several
years ago by saying, "It's a terrible thing to lose your
mind." The media howled. But, I noted it was a nervous
howling.

We are a nation obsessed with facts, information, and
the intellect. As I prepared for this sermon, it struck me
anew that Jesus requires a suspension of the intellect as
he calls those first four disciples. He later says to love the
Lord thy God with all your "heart, soul, *mind*, and
strength," but reasoning apparently had little or nothing
to do with this first call. Whether Jesus was a complete
stranger *in fact* or not, the text wishes the reader to
assume exactly that. There is no evidence that these four
knew anything at all about Jesus before he walked up
and said, "Follow me." His authority and truth would be
revealed later, on the way. This realization was a great
insight for me after reading the very intelligent, rational,
reasoned responses from this test group.

"[This sermon] does not fit into my belief system at all.
It scares me! Pre-war Germany . . . Charlie Manson . . .
Christ?" Though I laughed at this when I read it, such a
response reveals a very real reticence for individuals to
begin the Christian journey without full disclosure

beforehand of where they're going. We normally trust the mind over divine mystery.

Most people in the group accused me of taking this text too "literally." "[Your approach] suggests some kind of 'superman' effect that Jesus may have had in his voice or bearing and may tend to confuse faith with magic." One person felt compelled to remind me: "The account in the Bible of Jesus' recruitment of disciples is greatly abridged. We have no record of the polemics that precede this." Another was convinced that I "made too much fuss concerning the 'fact' that Peter and Andrew left to follow Jesus without knowing him. There is a lot that we do not know about Jesus. How do we know that Andrew and Peter did not know him?"

These responses raise several important questions that a congregation must continually address with serious seekers. Namely: what kind of book is the Bible?[4] What is the nature of narrative and how does it function in a faith community? What is it doing to the listener in the form we have inherited it? What responsibility does the preacher have in debunking an obviously mythological pericope? "It has always been hard for me," said a group member, "to grasp the total idea behind the stories, because of the fact that they seem like an old version of science fiction! How can anyone believe in some of the stories related in this book?"

These responses have revealed much to me about the skeptic in all of us, but particularly the adult who is returning to church for Christian formation leading to conversion. We need to talk candidly of this mysterious Christ that cannot be totally figured out or understood before the journey begins. We need to speak more openly of the Christ who *has* been revealed to faithful disciples who are down the road with him, loyally following, including the specific nature of the revelation. We cannot know everything there is to know about Jesus before choosing to follow. Initially, he is largely a stranger revealed to us in layers as we submit to his call. It is impossible to convince someone of Jesus' truth in the lab by rational propositions. One must embark, however tentatively. As Uncle Screwtape reminds his junior devil/nephew Wormwood in C. S. Lewis' *The Screwtape Letters*, "Merely to over-ride a human will . . . would be for [God] useless. He cannot ravish. He can only woo."

How might Christian sermons speak to the wide twenty-first century gap between divine call and our halting, intellectual response? Walter Brueggemann observes that "There was a time, perhaps 250 years ago, when the Christian preacher could count on the shared premises of the listening community, reflective of a large theological consensus. There was a time, a very long time ago, when the *assumption of God* completely dominated Western imagination, and the Holy Catholic Church roughly uttered the shared consensus of all parties. That shared consensus was rough and perhaps not very healthy, but at least the preacher could work from it."[5] I hardly need to state the obvious: such a "time" is long gone. New, creative models of preaching are needed to reach a newcomer who may very well hold an "assumption" of entrenched agnosticism as they walk in the door. Preachers who ignore such doubt will not be heard for very long. Sermons might effectively function just like this old story from a Capernaum fishing village—inviting a listener to take those first tentative steps of obedience behind a man who knows where he's going. Doubt is perhaps an inherent part of this journey, even as we leave our nets and fall in line, not quite sure of the destination.

Woody Allen, who plays the lovable and angst-ridden Boris Dimetrivich in the film *Love and Death*, faces a dark night of the soul on the evening before a duel that he is sure to lose. Boris, a reluctant soldier in the Russian Revolution, desperately wants to believe God will be with him. "If only God would give me some sign. If He would just speak to me. One sentence, two words. If He would just cough."

Two words? At least they're clear enough: "Follow me."

CHAPTER SIX

Learning to Preach from a Pew of Agnostics

At the end of the millennium, and of a century that has the Holocaust at its center, the reasons for doubt in God's existence are so easily come by—His invisibility, His apparent indifference to the torrents of pain and cruelty that history books and the news media report, the persuasive explanations that science offers for all phenomena once thought mysterious—that church attendance must be taken . . . as a willful decision to evade what G. K. Chesterton called "atheist respectability."
—John Updike[1]

This was a fascinating test group for me. I am profoundly grateful for the candor of these fourteen skeptics and their willingness to listen and respond so generously. I offer the following reflections and learnings for other preachers who sense value in using sermons to dialogue with newcomers to church life who are somewhere in between a mind-set they're leaving and a new world they're discovering, or even those skeptical church members who faithfully fill the pews each Sunday morning, holy doubts in tow.

(1) *Clarifying confusion concerning biblical narrative.* Throughout the project (underscored by the fourth sermon, but an issue from the outset) I sensed the group's misunderstanding of the need for, and nature of, biblical story. This misunderstanding is not unusual. Many modern people are preoccupied with factual historicity and are bewildered when a Bible story is taken seriously. "So pervasive is the penetration of biblical religion in our

culture," claims Richard John Neuhaus, "that even atheists are not generic atheists but Christian or Jewish atheists. That is to say, it is biblical religion that defines what
they reject."[2] Stephen Dunn describes this rejection well
in his poem, "At the Smithville Methodist Church,"
where two agnostic parents struggle with whether to
send their little girl to the local vacation Bible school:

> . . . soon it became clear to us: you can't teach disbelief
> to a child,
>
> only wonderful stories, and we hadn't a story
> nearly as good . . .
>
> Evolution is magical but devoid of heroes.
> You can't say to your child
> "Evolution loves you." The story stinks
> of extinction and nothing
>
> exciting happens for centuries. I didn't have
> a wonderful story for my child
> and she was beaming. All the way home in the car
> she sang songs,
>
> occasionally standing up for Jesus.
> There was nothing to do
> but drive, ride it out, sing along
> in silence.[3]

The modern agnostic seems to allow no middle ground
between searching for Noah's Ark on Mount Ararat and
punting the story entirely. "My daughter doesn't know
Moses from Goliath, but at least she grew up without
guilt."[4]

The preacher, of course, must not shy away from intellectual honesty. Wading through the theological implications of Abraham's seemingly bizarre offering of Isaac,
for example, is always going to be a bit tricky, no matter
the symbolic explanations of the story. At the same time,
excessive "explaining" of a story robs the narrative of its

power to shape and form faith *all by itself.* Many post-modern people are suspicious of a creeping fundamentalism in which the biblical words are seen as a sort of magic. Preaching must confront another sort of fundamentalism in which the power of story always plays second fiddle to rigid "fact." Sermons must try to reveal another world for people who are paid to bother only with the measurable and the observable—folk who long ago left narrative behind in the nursery. Says Puddleglum the Marshwiggle to the queen of the underworld in one of C. S. Lewis's tales about Narnia: "Suppose we *have* only dreamed, or made up, all those things—trees and grass and sun and moon and stars and Aslan himself. Suppose we have. Then all I can say is that, in that case, the made-up things seem a good deal more important than the real ones. I'm on Aslan's side even if there isn't any Aslan to lead it. I'm going to live as like a Narnian as I can even if there isn't any Narnia."[5] Sermons can point to the reality of God's kingdom, but can never produce proof or demand blind allegiance. We can only "woo."

Morris Dees, director of the Southern Poverty Law Center in Montgomery, Alabama, visited nearby Emory and Henry College a few years back and recalled one of his elementary school teachers who was never shy about preaching her message of temperance and the evils of alcohol in class. Morris remembered raising his hand. "But Mrs. Brown—just last week you told us that Bible story of Jesus turning water into wine at the wedding in Cana." A lengthy pause ensued as the teacher mulled over the clashing implications of her answer. "Well, Morris, we'd have all thought better of him if he hadn't done that." Many modern skeptics have been taught to use Bible stories in just this way (I realize this is mildly ironic given the rigid stance of this teacher). The "truth" for many skeptics resides in "facts" and when the facts don't jibe with one's belief system the story is disregarded as having any real power to guide one's life. This is rather sad to me since the Bible itself interprets Bible stories on levels other than the purely literal (see, for example, how the author of 1 Peter 3:18-22 reinterprets the Noah story from a baptismal perspective). Those who always wish to read the Bible literally, conservative Christians or agnostic liberals, may be surprised that scripture itself uses these old stories in creative, fresh ways that are never static or wooden. This notion of "living" word is a basic, core area of clarification when conversing with most modern agnostics I have known.

"I am convinced," says Richard Rohr, "that much, if not most, of the modern neurosis is a direct result of a lack of a common, shared story under which our individual stories are written. As a result, our tiny lives lack a transcendent referent, a larger significance, a universal and shared meaning. Our common life is a 'dis-aster,' literally disconnected to the cosmic 'stars'. We look to the private psyche but it is just not big enough or connected enough to encompass human spiritual longing."[6]

(2) *Raising doubts about doubt.* I believe it was Dietrich Bonhoeffer who said it was often easier to discuss God with an agnostic than a committed church person. I discovered throughout this project that although these skeptics were not sure what they were looking for, they were eager to talk about it. In a wonderful interview with novelist Doris Betts, the interviewer asks: "It seems people are willing to bring cynicism only to matters of faith. But how do you get people to be cynical about disbelief, too?"[7] I love that question. This is a very good role for our preaching to play: to widen the range of a skeptic's questions to include the very assumptions they hold most dear—to creatively raise doubts about doubt.

"Perhaps my greatest breakthrough with regard to belief," writes Kathleen Norris, "came when I learned to be as consciously skeptical and questioning of my disbelief and my doubts as I was of my burgeoning faith."[8]

(3) *Striving for pastoral vulnerability.* In one of Peter De Vries's hilarious later novels, a local pastor and a resident atheist agree to a public debate. The whole town turns out to witness this spirited clash of worldviews. "They locked horns energetically and sometimes savagely over such things as Darwin, the testimony of fossils, the pagan derivations of Christianity, the reliability of the Scriptures."[9] The debate ends in a draw, but each contestant succeeds in convincing the other. The atheist becomes a Christian and the pastor becomes an atheist! Faithful preaching is rarely like a debate. But it should attempt to address diverse areas such as science and faith, the authority of scripture, and the role of tradition. Sermons will require a pastor's most disciplined and prayerful work. "To continue to believe in a silent God who on the face of it has abandoned us to our fate is a lot of work, hard work, even for those who know the whole story of God's mighty acts."[10] Preaching, then, will not shy away from spirited public dialogue and it must remain vulnerable enough to come under the scrutiny of those who reject the faith. As a close friend (who has no idea what I'm doing with my life) wrote in a recent letter, "[If there is a God in a world like ours], God does not deserve our respect. If He can change things and doesn't or won't, then I choose not to respect him." We preachers need to discover how those outside "the choir" hear the Sunday sermon and mainstream Christian thought. "To an atheist," writes Wendy Kaminer, "the sacraments are as silly as a séance."[11] I need to know something about the newcomer who slipped in late and left early, her first time in church in thirty years. In fact, she just might be

my most important homiletical ally. Blessed is the pastor fortunate enough to befriend a few honest skeptics willing to offer observations of the world from their unique perspective.

(4) *Avoiding pulpit preachments.* Few people change from scolding. Sermons work best when the listener is invited to participate actively in the sermon's aim, questions, and resolution, usually completed outside the worship space, perhaps always open-ended and unfinished. Skeptics enjoy a challenge to dig. Listeners may not all arrive in the same place, but surely uniformity in response is not what we're striving for. In a recent sermon on the healing of the paralytic (Mark 2:1-12) I focused on the four guys who got their good friend in to see Jesus, ignoring various barriers. How they climbed on the roof (no small trick, I'd say, carrying a palsied man up a ladder). How they dug through the sod until soil sprinkled on Jesus' new coffee table. How they grinned and shyly waved at the astonished crowds who looked up through the hole in the ceiling. And how they lowered their friend with ropes right into the middle of our Lord's sermon. The story seems to be asking, "What am I willing to *dig through* to get to Jesus?" Jesus offers humanity a great gift. But often, we must dig for the treasure. Sometimes it's served up on a platter. Often it's not. Skeptics are usually very willing and eager to do some serious theological digging. "Doubts," says Frederick Buechner, "are the ants in the pants of faith. They keep it awake and moving."[12] Too many Christians, I fear, get forever stuck in a "sandbox" mode of digging and never venture out onto the roof where it's a little dangerous. Taking a cue from Jesus, pastors must invite "diggers" right into the middle of our sermons. I, after all, am not the only person in the Sunday assembly who has experienced the laying on of hands. Baptism is the primary and

central "ordination" of the priesthood of all believers. The priesthood of all skeptics needs to witness the valuable wrestling with God's word inherent in any serious believer.

(5) *Dealing head-on with the reality of suffering.* The eighth verse of the fifth chapter of the Letter to the Hebrews is one of those verses that must be read again and again before it begins to make any sense at all. "Although he was a Son, he learned obedience through what he suffered." What a marvelously liberating phrase. Jesus did not pop out of Mary's womb preprogrammed. Jesus learned about the meaning of life when he decided to enroll in the school of suffering—his own suffering and the suffering of others. Go figure. "You know, pastor," people sometimes tell me, "I would not choose to get cancer, but I sure have learned an awful lot about myself and my faith by dealing with it." "It was not until I cared for my mother, an Alzheimer's patient for many years," a loving son once told me, "that I finally understood why we need a cross hanging in the middle of our worship space, a cross that also marks our physical bodies in baptism." You may have a diploma from the finest university in the land, but the Bible says you really haven't been to school at all until you matriculate in the school of suffering. "It's time to stop fleeing from suffering, time to stop pretending we can avoid it. As we do, we will deepen and grow and find life. Beautiful people who've had easy lives and lots of money are usually about as deep as pie pans."[13]

Pastors are well aware, I'm sure, that this biblical claim simply sends many modern people into theological orbit. Almost every member of my test group cited the reality of suffering in the world as a major stumbling block to faith. Pastors often attempt to explain the persistence of suffering philosophically. For example, we might say

that the powerful emotion of compassion is not physical-
ly possible without the reality of suffering in the world.
And without compassion, we would be fundamentally
less than human. I believe that little conundrum to be
true in my head, but on my worst days it isn't all that
emotionally satisfying in my gut. "None of us has ever
seen this being," writes a former Presbyterian elder
turned atheist. "None of us has ever heard him, except in
the silence of our own heads. If I told you I had a friend
I had never seen or spoken with, who was invisible,
inaudible, and unverifiable, you would think I was
afflicted with an overactive imagination, if not by out-
right insanity. But if I told you I believed in God, you
would think I was perfectly sane. You have no reason to
think there is such a friend, and I have no reason to think
there is such a God."[14] Many caring people leave the
church and lose their faith because these old questions
are not adequately answered or even entertained by congregational leaders.[15] Raising regular questions about the
nature and purpose of suffering from the pulpit may give
others the freedom to raise questions of their own. Let
preachers forever recall God's words to Eliphaz the
Temanite toward the end of the book of Job: "My wrath
is kindled against you and against your two friends; for
you have not spoken of me what is right, as my servant
Job has" (42:7). You will recall that these three "friends"
encouraged Job to remain silent, confess the sin that originally caused his woes, and swallow his difficult questions in the midst of profound suffering. Job encounters
mysteries that questions can never answer in chapter 38,
but the reader is left with the distinct impression that
Job's honest ponderings have left him far closer to the
truth than Eliphaz, Bildad, or Zophar, well-intentioned
messengers of conventional religious wisdom.

(6) *Finding common ground.* I was pleasantly surprised

by how much I had in common with these fourteen skeptics. They all had a nose for exposing and lampooning religious kitsch. We live in a world where public figures say idiotic things (forgive me, Jesus) in the name of God. St. Louis Rams wide receiver Isaac Bruce had this to say, for example, after catching the winning pass in the 2000 Super Bowl: "That wasn't me. That was all God. I had to make an adjustment on the ball, and God did the rest."[16] (Except maybe cash the winning paycheck.) Sometimes I wonder if the greatest hurdle to faith in a postmodern era might be the "Christian" inanities spilling forth from the mouths of Christ's ambassadors. I realize this is a fairly judgmental thing to say in print. But for the sake of those feeling distanced from the church, perhaps it is high time to expose Christian drivel and share in skeptical repulsion that drives thinking folk away from church at an early age. All the skeptics in my group brought with them damaging religious baggage from the past. It is not easy to forget or shake loose from such baggage. The pulpit can be a place to find common ground with those who were forced to leave their minds at the door of the church at an early age, even when Jesus encourages the use of such as a locus for loving God (Mark 12:30).

In working with my group of fourteen, I learned about many hurdles that stand between Christianity and a large segment of our culture. William Willimon and Stanley Hauerwas once wrote: "Without God, all we have left is sentiment, a saccharin residue of theism in demise. Sentimentality is the way our unbelief is lived out."[17] I'm not sure I totally believe that after working with this group. Their "kind" are honest and gracious teachers for any pastor serious about linking authentic evangelism to the pulpit. For preaching is one way to address the concerns confronting many who are returning to congregations, looking for something but having many questions, healthy doubt, and genuine skepticism. Paul, who preached to his own share of agnostics, said it well: "After the secrets of the unbeliever's heart are disclosed, that person will bow down before God and worship him, declaring, 'God is really among you' " (1 Cor. 14:25). The preacher cannot take credit for a person's faith (or blame for lack of it). But the Sunday sermon can help reveal those hidden secrets Paul describes and lead a hungry inquirer to take a new look at the community of faith—a people formed by the Word at a place where the skeptical search for meaning intersects with biblical hope and honest confession: "God is really among you."

A friend got me aside after my work with this group concluded and said, "Now you know why many people stay away from church. It would be interesting to discover why others go at all." I now turn to how sermons shape the congregational newcomer and preaching's unique role in their welcome back to church.

Section II

CHAPTER SEVEN

Sermons and the Recently Returned

So this is what I tell people now: If you ever decide to go back to church, even despite yourself, you will eventually find yourself in a place where you can learn about mystery and timelessness. You will become part of a tradition of stories and verses and gossip greater than you can imagine. Circling and turning with a carnival of small-time saints, whose tales and homespun customs marshal wisdom out of a religious calendar, you will become a character, too, and a player in a cast.

—Gary Dorsey[1]

Congregations lucky enough to welcome back people like Gary Dorsey are surely blessed. Dorsey spent a year with a Congregationalist church in New England with the intent of objective reporting, but wound up experiencing much more. He gives the reader of his book a marvelous, almost week-by-week account of his conversion and reflections upon his life of questioning. But, Dorsey also gives an insider like me a candid outsider's perspective on church people. One hears his thoughts about the peculiar nature of the Sunday assembly, local organizational structure, small groups, and stewardship drive. This is rare in conversion literature. Usually we hear a convert's struggles with Jesus or God. Dorsey treats us to more: how God's people look and seem to act to the newcomer. His book helped me get into the minds of those, like my second test group, who have recently returned to congregational life. These days, when seekers come our way, I take my cue from Dorsey and say, "Spend a year with us." This gives a newcomer a chance not only to scratch the surface of a community, but also to mine the depths of a full seasonal cycle. The presence of seekers in or out of our catechumenal program has helped the whole congregation think about conversion and its ongoing nature in us all.

But what about sermons? Most preaching assumes in its listeners at least a cursory exposure to the basics of the faith. Sermons are shaped around stories many have heard before they could read. The preacher typically addresses a congregation which shares the Bible, a liturgy, basic theological tenets, and a common history. Even though a congregation may be quite diverse politically and sociologically, these shared Sunday reference points usually serve as the expected foundation from which a sermon emerges. "We may be different. We may not even like each other. But, by golly, we've got these things in common." How does a preacher address brand-new Christians or those returning to church for the first time since childhood, many of whom have not left the world of convinced skeptic that long ago, and who are probably still straddling a theological fence? There are many materials available on conversion, discipleship, and the changes a church must undergo to welcome new Christians.[2] But, what preaching considerations must a pastor reflect upon when a congregation receives numerous new faces with little or no Christian background?[3] Is a sermon with these folk in mind different from a sermon aimed at the fully assimilated? And what difference does that preaching make in their faith formation? These are not altogether new questions.

> There is perhaps no greater hardship at present inflicted on mankind in civilized and free countries, than the necessity of listening to sermons. No one but a preaching clergyman has, in these realms, the power of compelling an audience to sit silent, and

be tormented. Let a professor of law or physic find his place in a lecture room, and there pour forth jejune words and useless empty phrases, and he will pour them forth to empty benches. But no one can rid himself of a preaching clergyman.[4]

Anthony Trollope's fiction (1857) must have been born out of his own Sunday morning suffering. Is it possible for the sermon to actually shape and play a role in the ongoing conversion of God's people, particularly people returning to church after an absence of some length? Exactly how does this happen?

Working with eight "returnees" (sign maker, school librarian, speech therapist, attorney, crisis counselor, stay-at-home mom, environmental engineer, and child protection advocate), I set out to discover how reactions of these eight seekers to four sermons might reveal key areas of reflection for our ministry at St. John and the work of pastors in other locales. This group differed considerably from the skeptics group in that I met regularly with the seekers for purposes of planning, *lectio divina* Bible study on the assigned lectionary texts, common prayer, and sermon evaluation the following week. They became true partners in the preaching event. I highly recommend this practice in your own congregation and can think of no more practical discipline to expose a preacher to the concerns and needs of those returning to church.

After gathering the group for the first time and describing the process, it was especially important for me to learn about the various theological backgrounds which had shaped each group member for good or ill. I posed two questions: (1) Did you grow up in a religious tradition? If so, briefly describe that tradition and why you chose to leave it as a younger person. (2) What factors have led to your reconsideration of church at this point in your life? A sampling of their answers:

I grew up in the Southern Baptist tradition or lack thereof. I gradually drifted from my parents and church because I couldn't rectify the dogmatic gaps in the Baptist faith with the tools of mind-body-spirit that I had been culturally endowed with. I rebelled, turned to drugs, rock-n-roll, esoteric mysticism, and chugged huge cut-glass pitchers of cheap grace. I reconsidered the church at this juncture the way a person in a small row boat approaching Niagara Falls might consider an island protruding upward into my clandestine path.

I grew up in a nominally Methodist faith although the inclinations of my parents and grandparents seemed to differ little from the local conservative Baptists. I left the church at a time in my life when I viewed many things as half-empty rather than half-full. It was my perception that organized religion was simply a means whereby unscrupulous people exert temporal power over those they can persuade to believe the "party line." I still believe that every denomination is that way to one degree or another.

When I was a young child, my mother, siblings and I occasionally attended church. By the time I was about ten years old, we had all but stopped going. I always wanted to be baptized, but having my own children caused me to reconsider church.

I grew up in a fundamentalist church that preached this basic message: repent or die into a life of eternal damnation. I stopped attending church as a young adult, though I continued to seek spiritual growth through reading and prayer, trying to meld Eastern and Western religious teachings. I have become increasingly concerned about "evil" in the world. Jesus' teachings offer answers to my questions of how to respond.

My parents dropped out of the church when we moved once, and certainly never encouraged me to return on my own. Philosophy courses in college engendered a skeptical bent in me which took a while to straighten out. I've now returned to church due to a desire to live a more authentic life, confronting the absurdities and finality of death and life, wanting also to share that experience with others.

I grew up Roman Catholic, though I'm not sure I was ever connected enough to leave it as I have always probably viewed it as outside of me. First, my children have led me back to church. Second, I'm aware of a spiritual emptiness, a lack of centeredness or inner peace.

I was raised Presbyterian but don't recall a particular "tradition," mostly just how the church operated. I simply left it after leaving home as a teenager. Children, re-questioning and the need for spiritual answers, community and the possibilities that church offers, and being invited were all factors in my return.

I attended the Lutheran church regularly until I was about 17. My parents moved about 25 miles away from the church. I didn't ask my parents to take me. During college I became even more distant. Church lost its attractiveness. I've said before that there was a void in my life—both personal and family life. I needed the church. I wanted my family to experience a church community. I pray a lot these days, privately and with my family.

During the planning and evaluation of each sermon, issues of departure and return were quite central. Some members of the group dropped out of church earlier in life due to indifference; others tried to flee the religious wounds imposed by church leaders; still others experienced a crisis in faith spawned by maturing philosophical reflections—church did not fit their worldview. Although members of the group left for a variety of reasons, their return was marked by several shared needs: a spiritual "void" or "emptiness" that led to "re-questioning" and "confronting life's absurdities." Throughout our time together, individual histories sometimes shaped the conversation. That was good and needed. But it was largely the common bond of *returning* that caused members to truly come together as a group. They were on a shared spiritual journey that had brought them to this time and place. All four sermons were based on Old Testament texts dealing in turn with reconciliation, creation, exile, and call. Many came away with a renewed appreciation for long ignored parts of the Bible, now a surprising source for ongoing conversion.

With the following sermons, try to imagine someone relatively new to your congregation who has returned to church after a long absence. Try to listen with their ears. What has brought them to your doorstep? How might they be hearing this strange new language of Christ's church? What theological issues are important for them at this point in their faith development? How can your own preaching begin to address some of these issues from the pulpit on Sunday mornings?

As I did in Section One, I will follow each sermon with personal and group rationale explaining the choice of certain directions in the resulting shape of the sermon. Group members will then be allowed to speak their minds and describe the role of the sermon in their ongoing faith formation and understanding. Finally, I will venture to offer several considerations for pastors who wish to preach with this group in mind.

I was in our local video store not too many Sunday evenings ago, looking for a movie to rent—nothing in particular, just a cheap date. "Get something romantic or funny," my wife always tells me on the way out the door. I am the dark, sinister sort who loves twisted, complicated plots. So, I have to be reminded, often bringing home a darkly comic compromise.

A portly man and I change positions in front of the new release offerings. We share just the merest amount of eye contact. I must have smiled. He has an opening. "Have you ever seen *Carlito's Way*, man?" It takes a moment for me to realize that the question is directed at me. I admit to ignorance and turn away, moving down the aisle. "Oh, *man*," he continues, following me now, ignoring my hint to avoid conversation. "That's my all-time favorite movie. I just love Pacino. Oh God, Pacino just makes me . . . " And here he trails off and closes his eyes, a face full of utter bliss. I suppress the urge to run out of the store. I move away slowly. He follows. "Promise me," he says, "promise me that you'll rent *Carlito's Way* tonight." His eyes are wild. I make no such promise, but do pledge to rent it in the near future, just to end the contact and get away from this guy.

A few minutes pass. I remember Cindy's instructions, but all the romance and comedy titles look bland and insipid. A voice approaches from behind. He's beaming and notices that I'm still empty-handed. "Let me help you find it. Let me help you find *Carlito's Way*, man. You've got to see it." I laugh out loud. He's really a rather likable fellow.

I leave the store without Pacino going out into the Sunday night. Looking back through the glass exit door, I see him. With much animation, he's chatting with another potential convert, passionately telling his story, his experience. His eyes are closed. His face is full of bliss, transformed by what he shares, as if he's actually living the story in the present.

The reason I love working with seekers returning to church has something to do with that encounter in our local video store. In seekers there is often a passion for discovering Jesus that is often missing in more established church members. If we are not willing to help channel and satisfy this spiritual passion, seekers will go elsewhere. Churches who treat seekers like any other "letter of transfer" membership are missing a marvelous opportunity to share Christ and share in the congregational transformation that comes about when the Christian faith is fully assimilated into the life of a new convert. We cannot help catching their enthusiasm.

I am grateful for those spiritually thirsty newcomers who have graced our church doors. They are on a journey and are willing to talk about it. They have lived a good chunk of their adult lives and realized that something wasn't working. Surely, a basic pastoral assumption must be the following: the Holy Spirit brings seekers to our places of worship for a reason, not just to admire our lovely sanctuaries. If we're open to the Spirit, and open to the spirit of passionate curiosity that seekers bring, we'll help them discover exactly who has brought them to church and why. Preaching, perhaps easily overlooked as a resource for discovery and discernment given the modern Pandora's box of "spiritual" possibilities, is one of the more valuable pastoral gifts at our disposal in this exciting Spirit-inspired enterprise of ongoing conversion for adults finding their way back to the Body of Christ. There is no telling who might walk into our churches on any given Sunday with a spiritual yearning at least as great as that portly man filled with a passion for Al Pacino.

CHAPTER EIGHT

Payback Time

A Sermon for the
Sixteenth Sunday After Pentecost

Realizing that their father was dead, Joseph's brothers said, "What if Joseph still bears a grudge against us and pays us back in full for all the wrong that we did to him?" (Genesis 50:15)

In a recent installment of "Kudzu" in the Sunday comics, Pulitzer prize-winning cartoonist Doug Marlette depicts the Reverend Will B. Dunn addressing his congregation from the pulpit. The preacher is grinning and waving a piece of paper in the opening panel. He looks out over the top of his glasses and says to his flock, "Okay, Gang, Pop Quiz!" The Reverend Will B. Dunn is obviously pleased with himself. "Brothers and sisters," he says, "today I want to give you a test—a spiritual maturity test. This test will measure your depth of spiritual development as a congregation. Okay, ready? First question—Complete this sentence: 'Whosoever will smite ye on your right cheek . . . ' " And without hesitation the congregation thunders back, "WASTE 'EM! CLEAN HIS PLOW! SUE HIS CARCASS! STRING 'IM UP!" The last panel shows a depressed Reverend thinking these words to himself: "I may be forced to grade on the curve."

Regardless of what Jesus says on this matter, the practical reality is that we live in a world of paybacks and revenge. Eye for an eye, tooth for a tooth. A tit-for-tat life. We Lutherans may talk a lot about grace, but our world is ruled by retribution and revenge. You can forget about getting elected in the country these days if you're perceived as being "soft on crime." People should get what they have coming to them. What they deserve. Payback time. An offense is met with an appropriate punishment. When people say "justice was served" this is usually what they mean and have come to expect.

The next time someone is sentenced to be executed in Richmond in a capital punishment trial, notice the comments in the paper from those who applaud the verdict. "Now I can sleep. Now I can get on with my life. Now I'm at peace. He got what he deserved." Politicians left and right may say that the death penalty is primarily necessary as a "deterrent to crime." That's the party line. But let's be honest. We legally kill people in this country not to keep them off the streets, and not to make other criminals think twice. We kill people because they have killed others. Payback time. As a Christian, I'm vehemently opposed to the death penalty. But, I might have more respect for a politician who just comes right out and tells the truth. If our governor would say: "We are executing this person tonight because he deserves to die for what he did."

We live in a world of paybacks and punishment. That's just the way things work in matters large and small. *This* is our country's real saving gospel, if we came clean with our true feelings. Jesus' teachings are nice, but come on. Don't you think he was a bit naive? We know the gospel of Jesus. But there is another, powerful gospel at work in our lives—the gospel of getting even.

The story of Joseph, indeed the book of Genesis, ends today with his brothers fearing a payback. "What if Joseph pays us back in full for all the wrong we did to him?" The brothers throw themselves at Joseph's feet. They throw themselves on his mercy, but they are afraid. They oughta be. Genesis is full of dysfunctional families.

But these brothers, Jacob's boys, might just take the cake for criminal activity. Jealousy turns to violence early in the story. You remember. Joseph becomes his father's favorite son. He's got the coat of many colors, the ability to interpret dreams, and his father's eye. Then things turn ugly. Tending flocks away from dad, the brothers see Joseph coming and plot to kill him. As I recall, fratricide still pulls a jail term with most judges. Cool heads prevail, though. They throw him into a deep, waterless pit instead. What thoughtful brothers. Simple assault and battery can get you 5-to-10 in some counties. But during lunch, these quick-thinking entrepreneurs watch some slave traders heading to Egypt and recognize a business opportunity when they see one. They fish their brother out of the hole, sell Joseph into slavery, and take his bloody coat to dad with the lie of a wild animal story. Murder. Assault and battery. Kidnapping. This is what Joseph's brothers were capable of. Nice guys. Guys with long records you might see on a post office wall somewhere.

Today's lesson picks up with the dysfunctional family reunion. Ever been to one of those? Famine has driven the brothers into Egypt and the very guy in charge of the food bank is you-know-who. Joseph is the boss man. He's the head honcho, the exslave now in charge with privilege and power. And groveling before him are the very brothers who roughed him up so long ago. Now, isn't this rich? Payback time. Let 'em squirm awhile like worms on a hook. True to character, the brothers make up a lie about their father's deathbed plea for Joseph to grant sibling pardon. Jacob never says that before he dies, by the way. These pathetic brothers, aware of their past behavior toward the man in charge, know the jig is up. Like us, they lived in a world of paybacks and punishment. They are waiting for the hammer to fall.

Joseph then does a very strange thing. It's true that he doesn't seek retaliation. That's noble. But, neither does he say, "Aw shucks, guys, I forgive you. Don't y'all worry about that none. Get up and let's all do a group hug." No. Joseph weeps. Maybe Joseph is just sad because he senses his brothers haven't really changed all that much. Maybe he truly is glad to see them after all these years, in spite of that. But Joseph says something here that leads me to believe his tears are also on another level.

"Am I in the place of God?" Joseph asks. Note that this question comes at the very end of the book of Genesis, a book spilling over with deceit, murder, rape, thievery, infidelity and almost every sin the human race has ever concocted. It's easy to judge the people of Genesis. Joseph has every right to act upon the sins of his brothers. But he doesn't. He doesn't because he knows that the human payback system leaves him playing "God" and cuts his brothers off from the grace and redemption of the true God. Joseph weeps at least partly because he knows his family needs to encounter the God who was working good even in the midst of their evil. A God who can overcome and change their evil ways even now. Joseph refuses to block this transforming redemption.

When a greatly-admired Evangelical Lutheran Church in America synodical bishop recently resigned after admitting clergy sexual misconduct, I thought his letter of resignation in *The Lutheran* magazine was just right: "Before I became bishop," he said, "I violated my accountability to the triune God, to the whole church and to my wife and family. I believe in the power of redemption that comes from confession and an earnest plea for forgiveness. As God has the power to redeem us through his grace, I humbly ask for your support and your prayers." This bishop spoke the gutsy truth. Only God has the power to redeem us.

We live in a world where horrible things happen. Where we wound each other deeply. It hasn't gotten a whole lot better since Genesis. But when we operate under a system of calculated paybacks to avenge wrongdoing in the world, we can effectively cut off a person from God's redeeming power. They are beholden to us and not God. Joseph knew this. He knew his brothers didn't need to bow down to him, but to God.

I recently learned something interesting about the Latin word for "mercy," which we use weekly in the Kyrie. *Eleison* literally means to "unbind." Our related English word "liaison" loosely means "bond." When Joseph showed mercy to his brothers, he literally freed them from the bondage of his judgment. "Am I in the place of God?" he wanted to know. We must ask this question humbly and often. In our families, in our communities, among those who hold public office and decide the fate of others.

We may live in a "payback" world that seeks vengeance. But there is only one God. One judge of us all. One redeemer of the human race.

Give thanks that the position is already filled.

Response to the Sermon

It's interesting to note how many actions of the brothers in the Genesis 50 narrative seem to assign divine qualities to Joseph. After their father's death, the brothers caucus, discuss their plight and the probable grudge, weep openly, lie, and throw themselves at Joseph's feet. "We are your slaves," they pledge. Twice Joseph tells them to "Fear not," the angelic promise, perhaps sensing that such awe is misplaced. The brothers come close to worshiping Joseph in this passage. He is keenly aware of his advantage and his brothers' great need.

With the scene so richly set from way back in Genesis

37, the preacher is reminded of the system of paybacks and revenge that dominate our relationships. Few could blame Joseph for getting even with his brothers, or at least leaving them on the hook for awhile (he does seem to enjoy toying around with their emotions in chapters 42–44!). But, his question to siblings expecting retribution is the climax to this narrative if not the entire book: "Am I in the place of God?" Genesis is full of scalawags (Jacob's boys come by their behavior honestly) and unsavory characters who nevertheless are used by God for redemptive purposes. This question serves to remind a community that in our broken world, God is up to divine activity (Gen. 50:20) that subverts and even uses evil.

But more than that. When we've been wronged, our penchant is to hoard hurt feelings and revel in self-righteousness. We "lord" it over those who've wronged us. An apt word, "lord." We often hang on to these feelings because they perpetuate a Lord/subject relationship biblically reserved for God/humanity. Consequently, we wield "power" over another by withholding forgiveness.

Joseph seems to suggest here that idolatry is at stake. He realizes that his brothers truly need to do business with *God* instead of him. A key theological insight in my sermon preparation was the realization that forgiveness is ultimately important in this story, but not because it is "cleansing," or "moral," or "good for us." There is more at stake here. The radical forgiveness displayed by Joseph keeps him from breaking the first commandment, interrupts the cycle of paybacks, and brings infidels into the presence of the only thing that can truly change them (us): the judgment and grace of God.

The group agreed to read the entire Joseph narrative (a good chunk of Genesis!) in preparation for this sermon. We did an in-depth character analysis of the brothers' behavior and Joseph's strange response. This went well into the night. We talked at length about forgiveness and grace. My sermon theme of "paybacks" drew on several examples they provided, illustrating revenge as among the so-called sweetest of this world's feelings. This text opened several old wounds in people and raised the issue of whether or not humans can indeed block divine grace by nursing the wounds inflicted by others.

Barbara Lundblad notes that a sermon's occasional function is to "point out contrasts and dissonance between biblical vision and the realities of society."[1] In our congregation are a number of people who live more acutely in the "payback" world than most: attorneys, a police officer, and a juvenile detention worker. Many others are among the 80 percent of U.S. citizens who currently support the death penalty. Though Joseph's brothers committed no capital crime, they were certainly capable of such. It was important for me to establish how radical Joseph's question actually was in light of his brothers' behavior. This sermon attempted to convince a listener that because we have been dunked into the death and resurrection of Jesus, Christians will come to embody the subversive lifestyle of the cross. Seeing the world in a new way, through God's eyes as Joseph did, can be a painful new birth. Maybe our baptisms should come with warning labels. We "wet ones" are destined for trouble and controversy, if our conversion is authentic.

In response to this sermon, one group member wrote: "We (including me) must consume an inordinate amount of time just thinking up ways to get even or one-upping those who wrong us . . . we learn at an early age that retaliating is okay." Another said, "How tremendously difficult it is for those injured by unrepentant evil to let go of the desire for retribution. The image of grace as something constantly flowing from God, and which we can block or dam, is an image I had not thought of before and will hold on to." One very interesting slant that I had not considered was also offered: "The convincing point for me was the question, 'Am I in the place of God?' This is the clear beginning of exodus, the mirroring of Emmanuel, 'Don't be afraid. I AM in the place of God.'" A pretty advanced insight for a seeker who had been absent from church for more than twenty years!

A very helpful critique of the sermon emerged in the group evaluation session. It was pointed out that the grace and mercy element of the sermon could have been introduced earlier. What did the world of divine grace actually look like? The negative is often far easier to describe and make concrete. But what does grace look like? This seemed to be a felt need for both skeptics and seekers in this study.

Three main ideas surfaced after this first sermon: (1) There was genuine surprise that a perceived New Testament doctrine like "grace" was present so early in the Bible. "I am finding more examples of the principles, if not the coherent philosophy, of radical grace in the Old Testament." (2) The very concept of grace and how it works was still alien and strange for the group (this too concurs with my findings with the skeptics)—"I'm really trying to understand the concepts of mercy and grace. They don't fit into my belief system, but I'd like to try." Keep saying it: "Conversion is a *process*." (3) These old stories provide the *proper distance* to allow a listener to work on his or her own "stuff," recognizing elements of the biblical narrative in their own relationships. Without coming right out and naming a certain incident in the life of the seeker, the story uncovers the sin we have so expertly kept hidden.

"Sermons cannot do everything; possibly only jump-start our imagination, and that is enough."[2] This explains why parishioners' comments about a particular sermon may quite often be about ten different things, many not necessarily what you had in mind. The story has worked on individual imaginations in a variety of ways. One group member put it this way: "In some ways the sermon is like an inkblot where we project or fit our beliefs or views into the message. This sermon has caused me to evaluate my pettiness and slowness to forgive. Not forgiving cuts off both the transgressor and the victim from redemption."

These old stories, in which every word counts, cannot be preached straight at someone. They need time to sink in and to come at a person from a different, perhaps oblique, direction. "Tell the truth, but tell it slant," says Emily Dickenson in one of her poems. People new to the faith (and even some people in church every Sunday of their lives) cannot digest the many layers and density of timeless theological truths all at once. God's redemptive word, which will not return empty, has the power to kill and to raise folk from the dead. Remember—there may be casualties if we're about the business of the gospel. To leave one set of values for another is difficult and often painful. "The vast majority of people are sitting in the pews with parched lips. But one big gulp of Gatorade is not the answer. They will drown. Their thirst is so great that it requires a series of sips much like parched fields require a series of gentle rains."[3] In the lectionary cycle, sermons will eventually deal with potentially painful internal issues (but never in a pushy way) that seekers may have been running from all their lives.

> So if preachers or lecturers are to say anything that really matters to anyone including themselves, they must say it not just to the public part of us that considers interesting thoughts about the gospel and how to preach it, but to the private, inner part too,

to the part of us all where our dreams come from, both our good dreams and our bad dreams, the inner part where thoughts mean less than images, elucidation less than evocation, where our concern is less with how the gospel is to be preached than with what the gospel is and what it is to us.[4]

Friends who spent a year in Australia recently related that adult conversion is sometimes called "swapping over" on that continent. Sermons, I'm convinced, play an important part in the process of swapping stories (biblical narrative), swapping families of origin (baptismal identity), and indeed swapping our very lives for one utterly dependent on the gentle but unsettling Spirit of Christ. The seekers in this group were beginning to discover the risks and challenge inherent in such a swap, including the swap of the "payback" system for a life where only God is our ultimate judge and revenge is released and transformed in a new kingdom by the mystery and wonder of grace.

CHAPTER NINE

The Cosmic Choir

A Sermon for the
Twenty-first Sunday After Pentecost

*Sing to the LORD a new song; sing to the LORD, all
the earth. (Psalm 96:1)*

More than two decades ago, author Annie Dillard
spent a year in semi-solitude, living and writing along
the banks of Tinker Creek, two hours north near
Roanoke. That year produced a book that is fairly famous
among people who care about the natural world and its
mysteries. It has also become something of a modern
spiritual classic for people searching for the author of the
cosmos, the creative hand orchestrating the "music of the
spheres," as one hymn puts it. Though not writing overt-
ly about theology, Annie Dillard is a theologian. Listen:

> The mockingbird took a single step into the air and
> dropped. His wings were still folded against his
> sides as though he were singing from a limb and not
> falling, accelerating thirty-two feet per second,
> through empty air. Just a breath before he would
> have been dashed to the ground, he unfurled his
> wings with exact deliberate care, revealing the
> broad bars of white, spread his elegant, white-
> banded tail, and so floated onto the grass. I had just
> rounded a corner when his insouciant step caught
> my eye; there was no one else in sight. The fact of
> his free fall was like the old philosophical conun-
> drum about the tree that falls in the forest. The
> answer must be, I think, that beauty and grace are
> performed whether or not we will or sense them.
> The least we can do is try to be there.[1]

"His wings were still folded . . . as though he were singing from a limb and not falling." There is a creeping heresy among church people that assumes *our* praise, human praise, is really the main thing that pleases God and floats God's celestial boat. That if we pull ourselves out of bed and do "liturgy" on Sunday, even when we yawn or stumble through it in a groggy post-Saturday night stupor, we're doing God a colossal favor, and this will make the deity purr like a cosmic Cheshire Cat for another week. Songs to God are sung on Sunday, by golly. And by humans. In a church and for an hour.

Well, pardon me, but no. Way off. If you think such, that humans are responsible for the praise choir, then think again. And thank God we're not. Because most of the time we're so caught up in our own affairs and our own futures and our own little plans that we fall asleep even when awake and miss the song going on all around us every minute of every day. "Hosanna, Hosanna, Hosanna," sing the leaves and the stars and the mockingbird. "Beauty and grace are performed whether or not we will or sense them. The least we can do is try to be there." Which is another way of saying that we are invited to join a choir already in existence long before we were named. And a choir that will be singing long after we stop breathing. What a relief. What we do here on Sunday, and your personal wakefulness to the song during the week, strengthen the cosmic choir. But we're not responsible for the song. We might add to the volume, so that those really hard of hearing might have their ears unstopped. But, God does not absolutely depend on our voices. God has other sopranos, altos, tenors, and basses singing in every imaginable key. God transposes the music to fit the textures of this earth. "Sing to the Lord," says today's psalm. "Sing all the whole earth." Heavens rejoicing. Thundering seas. Joyful fields. Shouting trees.

Eclipsing moons. The psalm points our senses to a symphony of sound and sight. There's a concert around every corner.

Years ago, miners would keep caged canaries in their work areas. The birds would be lowered far below the surface of the earth, down the mineshaft, to monitor the quality of the air. If the birds stopped singing or got sick, the miners knew it was time to get to the surface. I suppose, however, that the birds also provided occasional comfort by offering song in a dark place. When God became incarnate in Jesus, God willingly took on the constraints of human flesh. Jesus lowered himself into the mineshaft called the cross so that others might live. The Easter surprise is that the song lives on. And nothing, not even death, can contain it. We can hear the song even in the darkest of places.

John Muir, the great naturalist who explored much of this country on foot in the mid-1800s, struggled with depression on and off during his life, and wrote in his journals that people mocked him for spending so much time wandering the countryside looking at weeds and blossoms. He was heartened time and again not by therapists, but by wild nature. Sitting by a stream in Tennessee, he was once serenaded by a tiny bird. "It had a wonderfully expressive eye," he noted in his journal, "and in one moment that cheerful confiding bird preached me the most impressive sermon upon heavenly trust that I have ever heard."

When we notice autumn leaves spilt like a box of crayons. When multicolored periwinkles burrow into the sand between our toes at the beach. When blueberries gush their sweet goodness past our tongues in late August. When cataracts and waterfalls bore geologic holes in a riverbed, joyfully gurgling away the millennia. When stars and planets sashay in the annual dance of earth's rotation. When a band of starlings bends and turns in the sky like a drunk Slinky. When we notice this song of which the psalmist speaks, offered up to the Lord and Author of the Cosmos, we are freed from our own worst enemy: self-absorption. Thinking we're such hot stuff and that everything of consequence depends on us. Joining this cosmic choir liberates us, finally, from narcissism—looking in the water and seeing only ourselves. "Sing!" we're told today. Sing! It's an imperative verb. Join the choir! Stay mum and you die. Strangled by the self.

Last April, my wife and I traveled to Mt. Pisgah near Asheville for our fifteenth wedding anniversary. The inn there is located in a unique ecosystem, about 5,000 feet above sea level. After a hard rainstorm one afternoon, we ventured up the trail at Fryingpan Gap, so named for the community pan hung on a tree used by mountain travelers heading west over the Blue Ridge. A fire tower punctuates the end of this trail. We climbed (how do you resist a fire tower?) and held on tight at the top, two hooded acolytes pummeled by wind, waiting for the show. God was frying up quite a feast for us at this gap. The clouds raced by, just below us, spilling over the ridge like milk over the lip of a cereal bowl. So fast, it was like they were being vacuumed. The sun was setting and played tag with the shadows in the hollows. We turned 360 degrees, clutching the iron rail for dear life. Again and again we turned, like kids in creation's candy shop, turning atop a fire tower, almost dancing. No words. But song, nonetheless.

"Beauty and grace," says Annie Dillard, "are performed whether or not we will or sense them. The least we can do is try to be there." And maybe one more thing, according to the psalmist.

Grab your pitch and sing along!

Response to the Sermon

A Copernican revolution is still waiting to happen in terms of humanity's relationship to the rest of the created order. With little argument from churches, humans largely believe that we are at the absolute center of the universe and everything else in creation revolves around and serves us. I recall a cartoon in *The New Yorker* several years ago where a portly man is looking out a bay window, admiring his vast holdings. The caption read: "God may have created it, *but I own it.*"

It isn't so hard for a preacher to make the false conclusion that earthly praise to the creator originates in (and is perhaps limited to!) human song. Thus the birth of the curious oxymoron, the "worship hour." Psalm 96 subverts this misguided anthropocentrism, of course, along with many other biblical passages. The psalmist takes great pains to suggest that the praise choir is much more expansive than most Christians confess. In fact, there is great comfort found in a cosmic choir that keeps singing around the clock independently of human effort. There is something greater at work here than our own fickle efforts at extolling the wonders of God. If we can't sing along, for whatever reason, we can listen as the old mysteries offer their diverse song. It's refreshing and a relief not to carry the tune alone.

In preparing for this sermon, the group of returnees spent a good deal of time examining the nature of psalms as liturgical, poetic prayers, unpacking all three words slowly. Laurence Perrine once noted: "Poetry should never be read from a hammock. It is not meant to soothe and relax, but to arouse and awake, to shock into life, to make one more alive."[2] We counted thirteen imperative verbs in this psalm meant to shake even the most hungover worshiper out of a Sunday morning stupor. The group was especially intrigued with Psalm 96 as a form of *prayer*. This was a new insight for some who had been raised with a "every head bowed, every eye closed" understanding of prayer.

The group was very helpful as they assisted in shaping the idea of "self-absorption" as it eventually appeared in the sermon, which turned on a repeated refrain, penned by Annie Dillard: "Beauty and grace are performed whether or not we will or sense them. The least we can do is try to be there." The sermon attempted to mirror the psalm in both structure and sense. One respondent noted that our self-absorption and narcissism "is the central issue that interferes with my commitment to and belief in God." Another noted that "I am often juggling work, family, special interests, and other activities and I don't take time to sit and think, reflect, and relax. Without such an opportunity I become complacent, almost insulated [from God's grace] by the daily routine."

"Has this sermon reshaped your understanding of prayer?" I asked on the response forms. "Recently," said one, "I began praying outdoors as often as weather and time permit—down by the river on Saturday morning. The Psalms have been a major part of my daily prayers and they really 'wake you up' when you sing them in a natural setting. You know, of course, that you are confronting that old heresy of gnosticism (antimaterial bias) that has always lurked about the mental fringes of the church." Another said: "I find myself 'singing a new song' [one of our hymns that Sunday] on a daily basis, and at times that are surprising to me." "I'm beginning to include a more 'outward' approach toward prayer instead of strictly inward." Finally: "I was surprised by the image of nature, the whole earth, literally singing praise and the notion that we humans may not even carry the lion's share of responsibility for prayers of praise. Too often I view prayer as a cloistered experience.

The sermon emphasizes that prayer can be offered outside of our artificial environments. It takes some of the pressure off if we can be prayerful even in silent wonder."

It takes some of the pressure off. If the first sermon with this group perhaps missed what grace in relationships actually looks like, the second afforded an opportunity to gaze at grace more concretely. This was a different type of grace than that described in the first sermon. Easier to paint. Because the psalm was so concrete, words could be chosen with imagistic accessibility in mind—mockingbird, choir, mineshaft, firetower. The project group seemed grateful for the vivid over the theoretical. "The lavish and delightful imagery made the sermon 'one with' the psalm. This sermon probably moved and opened me up more than practically any I can remember without heavy reliance on the intellect."

There is nothing like the majesty and grandeur of liturgy done well. There is nowhere I'd rather be on Sunday morning than finding refreshment and encouragement through shared word and sacrament. But, although Lutherans sing each week, *Holy, Holy, Holy, heaven and earth are full of your glory* (Isa. 6:3), church people might be lulled into believing that God is primarily found in a building on Sunday mornings. The Bible teaches us that God is revealed through an abundance of natural venues and phenomena. Stephen, whose stoning we recall each December, had it right. "The Most High does not dwell in houses made with human hands" (Acts 7:48). I strongly suspect there is a connection between this statement and his death at the hands of angry religious leaders.

This sermon addressed a felt need for "returnees" to develop a spirituality not limited to the interior of a church building, but centered on experience of God wherever one happens to be during the week. "For many modern Christians," writes Jay McDaniel, "Christianity is a text-based, creed-centered, human-preoccupied, indoor religion. Often our worship is symptomatic of the problem. It almost always occurs in an indoor setting, separated from the out of doors by stained glass windows and controlled temperatures. Our task, it seems, is to know the name of God's only begotten Son, but not the names of wild grasses or resident birds."[3] Seekers bring so much baggage when it comes to ecclesiastical authority and someone (usually clergy) trying to limit where God is found ("in church," of course!). According to Psalm 96, we kneel with the praise choir in a variety of places not limited to Sundays at eleven.

When we learn the song and become aware of its depth, breadth, and history, we are given courage to face anything life can throw at us. Kathleen Norris cites the strange story of a young girl who was killed with many other evangelical Christians in the village of El Mozote during the height of the Salvadoran war in 1981. The girl was raped and brutalized many times in the course of the afternoon. "Through it all . . . this girl had sung hymns, strange evangelical songs, and she had kept right on singing, even after they had done what had to be done, and shot her in the chest." The girl continued to sing, with blood flowing from her chest. The soldiers shot her again and still she sang. Becoming fearful, they finally "unsheathed their machetes and hacked through her neck, and at last the singing stopped."[4] The song of the ages is hard to kill, difficult to silence, impossible to completely wipe out. The song in the middle of that young girl's heart, according to Norris, is about a "love stronger than death, a love that shames us all."

When seekers learn the song, they are linked to Christians beyond time and space—the communion of saints. They are also joined to the whole cosmos, the entire created order, confidently offering up praises to God. "Then I heard every creature in heaven and on earth and under the earth and in the sea, and all that is in them, singing, 'To the one seated on the throne and to the Lamb be blessing and honor and glory and might forever and ever!' " (Rev. 5:13).

Here's a pastoral suggestion. Get your seekers to the choir practice of the cosmos as soon as possible, even if they can't sing a lick. It is here that we are freed from self-absorption, adding our voices to a song sung long before we were born. Perhaps listening for the song and finding our place in the choir is the very thing that eventually liberates us to love as Jesus loved.

CHAPTER TEN

Going Home to God

A Sermon for the Second Sunday of Advent

A voice says, "Cry out!" And I said, "What shall I cry?" (Isaiah 40:6a)

I remember. I remember a day-hike once taken in late July with a group of confirmation students returning home after a weekend retreat. We were walking along a stream in Backbone Rock Recreation Area, rounded a bend, and suddenly came upon a five-foot-long black-snake, just barely off to the side of the trail. But not just any blacksnake, mind you. This one was in the middle of a meal.

A semiswallowed chipmunk struggled for life in the snake's throat, half in and half out; the poor thing's legs still kicking and writhing to escape, much like a swimmer racing furiously into a turn.

We watched the scene both mesmerized and repulsed, unable to look away. Entranced. No words. Someone finally commented that maybe we could reach down and pull mightily and set Alvin, Simon, or Theodore free, but it was too late for that. The legs helplessly shrank before our eyes and the chipmunk's writhing gave way to the meal that it was—a large swollen blob in the reptile's flexible throat. Nature's way, you see.

I remember. I remember a man named Isaiah, called by God to comfort exiles on the banks of a river; exiles on the brink of extinction. "Cry out!" said a voice that meant it. And the reluctant prophet responded with his gut, as honestly as anyone on the verge of being swallowed could reply. "What shall I cry?" he wanted to know. What in God's name do you want me to say? he inquired of the heavenly imperative. That people get swallowed in due time? That we struggle and kick and blossom but finally get eaten by the big guy? What shall I cry? How do you expect me to "Comfort, O comfort" in a land like this, where the grass withers and flowers fade? Surely "all people are grass."

Our lesson this day from the book of Isaiah addresses a very specific event in Israel's life. God's people are in captivity—exiled and enslaved far from home in Babylon. Jerusalem, the invincible city and locus of divine activity, has been leveled. In spite of prophetic warnings that Israel was falling away from her roots and ignoring God's word, things seemed good for God's people and the economy was thriving.

But in 587 B.C., the Temple was burned by invaders, people were taken away in chains, and forcibly marched eight-hundred miles from home. This was seen as a sign of God's punishment. For close to seventy years, they would live as exiles. They would live with their guilt at having ignored God. They would live with the fact that they were being assimilated into a pagan people. They would live with the reality that the old ways, God's ways, were being swallowed by a foreign culture as the generations passed, like a snake making a meal of a chipmunk. God's people were on the verge of extinction. A hymn that we'll sing captures the national lament of people who have been enslaved in Babylon for generations: "Oh come, oh come, Emmanuel, and ransom captive Israel, that mourns in lonely exile here." The people had almost given up hope of ever returning home. They were being swallowed in exile.

God's announcement in Isaiah 40, spoken in heavenly assembly, is that the exile is over. God's people have learned a lesson and have been in Babylon long enough. "Comfort, O comfort my people, says your God." The Temple will be rebuilt. The exiles are coming home on a road through the wilderness.

Life is full of people who feel exiled; who feel like they're on the verge of being swallowed. I was once a summer chaplain for eighty high security inmates at a state prison in South Carolina. As I made visits around each rectangular tier, four and five stories above the floor of the main building, I'd notice arms reaching through bars, holding a small piece of broken mirror. Men would angle the mirror down the narrow walkway to see who was coming. I came to see that stretching, that desperate, angled reflection, as a metaphor for many of their lives— men who confessed to me that they knew they had done wrong, worried now that prison life was about to eat them alive, swallow them whole; wondering if they would ever make it home again.

But prison is not the only place you'll find exiles. They are all around us—people who are fighting addiction, enslaved to drugs or alcohol and unable to break free. People fighting depression and the heavy, isolating emotional toll that depression brings. People involved in abusive relationships, unable or unwilling to end them. It does not take much imagination to realize that we live in a land of many exiles, people who feel that life is just about over—who feel that their situation is eating them alive, that they are being swallowed. This time of year, the seasonal cheer blaring forth by way of mall Muzak only serves to remind many how life can be far from cheery.

And sometimes exile is far from obvious. Here in America, we live in a land of great religious freedom. We also live in a land of great excess and a multitude of false idols calling us away from the faith. I once heard a theologian say, "If you're an American and a Christian, you've got a problem." To be a person of God living in America often feels like living in Babylon. At every step of the way we are invited to assimilation and compromise, to trust in the false idols of prosperity, power, and affluence. To a Christian, living in a culture like ours will often feel like exile. America is *not* our true home.

Sometimes I think of that snake and chipmunk beside the stream at Backbone Rock. We live in a world where guilt, addiction, abuse, and even the dominant culture of this country can swallow us; can kill us. We lose our way—a roof over our heads, yes, but homeless nonetheless. You don't have to go to Babylon to feel exiled. Exiles are your neighbors, your coworkers, yourself. Us.

"Comfort, O comfort my people, says your God." A highway is built. The exiles, on the verge of being swallowed, are going home. Can we become a place where exiles gather? More and more, I see the church as a group of once-exiled people brought home. We come from different places, we can tell stories of various captivities, but what we all have in common is Jesus the liberator whose advent and invitation brings us to this table. "Welcome home," says the host.

He offers himself for the sake of this world and says to weary exiles dining at the table of God, "Swallow me instead." Body of Christ given for you. The exile is over. Welcome home. Welcome others.

Response to the Sermon

The popularity of Handel's *Messiah* notwithstanding, Isaiah 40 is a difficult text to preach. This passage is not a clean, camera-ready unit like a parable or psalm. Without some historical reference to the Babylonian Exile, including a link to a popular hymn, most modern seekers would miss the point of this poem entirely.

The preacher needs to ask basic questions such as, "Who's speaking? To whom? When?" It's easy to assume that the prophet speaks throughout the pericope. Not even close! If Isaiah doesn't speak until the middle of verse 6 (which I think is the case), then the first *prophetic* word in the passage isn't comfort but reluctance. Even sassiness and jadedness. "*What shall I cry! What do you want* me to tell these exiles in a land like this?" Isaiah is not the jaunty agent of God here, at least not at first. He is very close to giving up hope, resigned to the fate of faded flowers. Isaiah is not speaking to Israel's situation, but *out of it*. This greatly informed my decision to begin with an image of hopelessness rather than traditional comfort.

In short, this was a rather theologically and historically dense text to deal with in less than fifteen minutes. Maybe that's why I've skipped it before and opted for John the Baptist, whose message is as clear and concrete as camel's hair. Isaiah drew me, I think, because of the nature of this group—people returning to church after a time away. I did not deal with this specifically in the sermon and the analogy is not perfect compared with biblical exiles. But I hoped the issues raised in the sermon were close enough to stimulate reflection concerning their own "homecoming" and highway back to God.

The group wrestled with three questions: "What images come to mind when you hear the word 'exile'? Have you ever experienced an exile of sorts? What might be some modern experiences of the word 'exile' captured by the media?" We came up with about twenty specific images, including several for future sermons on the same text.

I thought a good bit about the actual shape of this sermon, wanting the image of "being swallowed" by a competing culture to serve as a bridge between biblical and modern exiles. I suspected they could find a pattern embedded in Israel's exile that might mirror their own experience of returning. "As much as anything else," says Frederick Buechner, "it is the experience of the absence of God that has brought them [to worship] in search of his presence."[1] A preacher dare not skirt around this sense of divine absence or diminish its importance in the emerging faith of a seeker. As one group member said of this text: "I think it suggests that we are consoled only after we are broken to the heart in our own exiles." Barbara Brown Taylor offers sage advice for those who preach in an era when God seems silent:

> Our duty in this time of famine is not to end the human hunger and thirst for God's word but to intensify it, until the whole world bangs its forks for God's food . . . Whatever preachers serve on Sunday, it must not blunt the appetite for this food. If people go away from us full, then we have done them a disservice. What we serve is not supposed to satisfy. It is food for the journey. It is meant to tantalize.[2]

In our group planning, we tried to get in touch with Isaiah's prophetic frustration with God's absence. I felt it was important to begin the sermon not with traditional joy and hopefulness (that was the heavenly announcement) but from the perspective of the exiles, mired in dismay with feelings of being swallowed whole in Babylon. This extended metaphor invited listeners to make their own creative connections with the past.

Again, I invoke the same point made earlier: these old narratives provide the proper emotional "distance" for a listener to expose his or her history to the healing inherent in the text itself. A preacher must respect that distance and not sledgehammer the point to make it too obvious lest the listener's insight is rushed prematurely before it can truly be heard and dealt with. There is something like holy percolation at work here. I think it was Fred Craddock who said sermons (when they work) leave bits of bread along the path, leading the listener along from here to there instead of spelling everything out. Our task is not an attempt to make all paradox perfectly clear. This realization is a key ingredient for formational preaching that shapes folk just returning to church. A pastor's tendency is to say too much in an attempt to be "helpful."

Ultimately, the text does the shaping (not the preacher) but the sermon awakens the boundaries and context in which change is possible. In Sunday worship, the preacher takes the ancient liturgical pattern and holds it up like a mirror to the week. We are the prodigal son or daughter, the wounded one in the ditch, Adam and Eve with our fingerprints all over that apple core, the exiles returning home. The drama continues with unlimited acts. The church year unfolds and measures time in such a way that inevitably draws us into the action. In baptism seekers are dunked into this old story, now new. It takes a while to learn to measure and mark time this way. Bill Gates is right, of course, even though he puts it rather crassly: "Just in terms of allocation of time resources, religion is not very efficient. There's a lot more I could be doing on a Sunday morning."[3] It will take quite a bit of time ("inefficient" time by the world's standards) to help seekers discover the power of the church year.

"The church can be home for exiles just like me," said one recently baptized person aware of her ongoing journey home. "The sermon," said another, "awakened the notion of my connectedness with fellow converts and to spiritual refugees throughout history. It aimed for the heart (or, given the metaphor), the gut of emotional and spiritual exile." Every member of the group found some connection. This was a sermon with an ellipsis at the end—to be continued in the minds of the listeners; not meant to be tied up with a neat bow. In a season where the church so often "cootchy-cootchy-coos" over a manger, I felt this text begged for an expanded understanding of the Savior who leads Christians home. The images in this sermon (snake, prison) are deeply archetypal. Perhaps only a Savior who knows about being swallowed and offers his life for the sake of a swallowed world can extend the liberating, paradoxical invitation that truly frees us.

I risked inverting the image of being "swallowed" toward sermon's end. "The connection of the eucharistic swallowing of the body and blood of Christ as liberation from the sense of being swallowed up by a culture at odds with our beliefs was dramatic and uplifting." But another wondered insightfully: "If being a meal [swallowed] is inevitable, and if Christ is a substitute meal, then what does that leave for me to do? I'm still struggling with an old belief system and trying to refashion a new one. Perhaps this is the question [for me] to answer: Once you've been saved, then what?" Though exceeding the limits of the text we worked with, this is an excellent question and connects back with the questions raised earlier: What does grace look like? Or, better still: What will grace evoke in a person or community? These are sanctification questions and to ask them after a sermon on exile is not bad evidence that the preached text has helped lead the listener in the direction of "home" but also towards a thirsting for the next step: ongoing life in the holy land called church—a life towards which God is constantly calling us ever more deeply and dangerously. Part of my pastoral prayer that day addressed such a call:

> Lord, so many images of exile fill your world.
> Refugees in Rwanda. Starving people in the Sudan.

Embattled neighborhoods in Bosnia. Strife in the inner cities. Poverty in these Appalachian hills. People are swallowed without headline or notice. But you have built a highway welcoming people home. Can we at St. John come to see ourselves as a rest stop on that great highway? Fling wide our doors this season, Lord, as we share joyful refreshment at your table—Advent fare for exiles like us returning home.

CHAPTER ELEVEN

Between Old and New

A Sermon for the
Second Sunday After the Epiphany

Samuel lay there until morning; then he opened the doors of the house of the LORD. Samuel was afraid to tell the vision to Eli. (1 Samuel 3:15)

Do you remember how Samuel the prophet was born? Dear me, he was a special baby. But he wasn't even supposed to be. Listen children, listen and I'll tell you how a child of God was born and how he came to be a great prophet.

Once upon a time there was a woman named Hannah. Now Hannah was a devout woman of faith with great trust in the Lord. But Hannah was sad. She was barren and childless. In our day alternatives to infertility exist, but in Hannah's world her inability to become pregnant caused her great pain, even public ridicule. A childless woman was perceived as one from whom God had withdrawn his blessing. So Hannah felt incredibly alone, no matter how much her husband tried to comfort her. People talked about her behind her back, wondering what she had done to merit God's displeasure.

One day, Hannah rose and walked to the temple. Tears streamed down her face. She poured out her heart to God. She prayed harder than she had ever prayed before. She prayed for a baby boy. And she promised to offer this child to the Lord as one set apart to do God's will, if only God would fill her womb. Hannah prayed so hard that day that Eli, the temple priest, thought she was drunk!

141

Sure enough, in due time Hannah conceived. And baby Samuel was born. When Samuel was weaned, Hannah kept her promise to God. She brought her child up to the temple, to the old priest Eli. Hannah said to the old man, "Remember me? I prayed for this child several years ago, and the Lord heard me. Now I'm keeping my promise. Here is Samuel. For as long as he lives, I'm loaning him out to the Lord."

Time passed. Eli and Samuel lived in the Temple together. Eli taught the boy all the priestly duties. They were like father and son—which was meaningful for Eli in his old age because his real sons had no regard for the Lord or their role as priests. They were an embarrassment to the family, rebellious. (I'm sure you know how some preacher's kids can be.) Eli's sons were wild, took an unfair share of the offering, and committed unspeakable, indecent acts with women right on the steps of the sanctuary! Scandalous. Eli had no control over them. They were wild hellions. Samuel may not have been Eli's real son, but he was certainly his spiritual son. Eli was the boy's mentor, a tutor in all things godly.

Well, one night, after the old priest laid his tired bones down for sleep, weary after another day of listening to prayers and settling disputes, Samuel appeared at Eli's bedside saying, "Here I am, for you called." Samuel so much wanted to please Eli, especially since his own sons never bothered. But Eli, half-asleep, said, "No, my son, I didn't call. Go on back to bed." In a half-hour, Samuel again trotted in obediently. "Here I am, for you called." Same response. And even a third time. Now Eli was old, but he wasn't dumb. Even though the word of the Lord was rare in those days, well this must be it. "Go lie down again," said the old priest. "If he calls you say, 'Speak, Lord, your servant is listening.' "

Well, Eli's hunch was correct. It *was* God. "Speak, for

your servant is listening," said the boy. Samuel was all ears that night. He couldn't believe what he was hearing. Eli, his spiritual mentor, his role model in the faith, was out as priest! And Samuel, only a boy, would be the new spiritual leader for God's people. It was too much. God said, "I am about to do something in Israel that will make both ears of anyone who hears it tingle."

Can you imagine how Samuel received this news? Can you guess what was rattling around in his young, obedient mind? Samuel stared at the ceiling until morning, bug-eyed, mulling over the implications of these words. He knew something that his own spiritual daddy didn't. So, he was afraid. Who wouldn't be? Samuel was afraid to spill the beans because he knew that once those words were out of his mouth everything would change. Samuel was standing smack-dab between the old guard at the Temple and the new life to which God was calling him. He was being called to replace the spiritual foundations that had raised him in the faith! Now Samuel knew his birth was special. But he could never have guessed how special. When Eli called Samuel the next morning, the boy said, "Here I am." Same words as the night before, but with a decidedly different inflection come daybreak.

Have you ever been privy to words that you knew *had* to be spoken? Words that you could not possibly keep quiet about but also words that will completely change everything as soon as they leave your mouth? That's a hard, excruciating place to be. And that's where Samuel was when daybreak came. Samuel was smack-dab between the old and the new and he was called to announce the end of an era and the coming of another. He was called to be a prophet, yet he was still a boy. Samuel was born unusually and he was called to help bring about unusual birth in Israel's staid, ineffectual life. Birth, of course, is always painful and Samuel was coming to grips with just *how* painful as he stared at the ceiling during that long, lonely, dark night of the soul.

What is true of Israel is also true of Christ's church. People are born unusually, we the baptized. God might just visit us in the Spirit and share a vision. Sometimes this vision comforts. But just as often in the church this vision disrupts. Those who speak the vision, in announcing something new, often stand precisely where Samuel stood. Jesus Christ stood there. Martin Luther King stood there. Dietrich Bonhoeffer stood there. Dorothy Day stood there. Oscar Romero stood there. They could not keep quiet about what they had seen and heard, but they also knew that speaking caused great turbulence.

When change occurs in the church, it is important for agents of change to feel something of what Samuel felt: the awkward tension between tradition and faithfulness. We need prophets in the church. But if we don't feel Samuel's tension acutely, then perhaps the prophetic vision is not authentic. Jesus wept over Jerusalem. Samuel surely wept for Eli.

I hope you see Samuel's predicament today. He is torn between the past to which he owes a debt and the compelling future towards which God calls. It is a hellish place to stand. He feels torn apart. God is always calling people to newness and that will involve pain. Samuel learned this one night long ago. He was destined at birth to live this way. And so it is with those born in baptism, "on loan" to the Lord from our watery beginnings. We stand between the past and the future, knees knocking, but hopefully available to what God is doing. "Here I am," we say.

God needs people to stand just where Samuel stood.

Response to the Sermon

The story of Samuel (on one level) is one of the most charming and sentimental tales in the Old Testament. A young boy is called in the night by God, but mistakes the call as being from his elderly mentor in the faith. Most readers only remember certain parts of the story—the happy ones. Our reading of young Samuel is like Noah's Ark and the Red Sea narrative in that way. Even the lectionary drafters encourage the preacher to cut off the story at verse 10 and not deal with what follows. We like to read the Old Testament selectively and with rose-colored glasses.

Sticking with the bare fact of divine visitation without dealing with why God has shown up in the first place (in a time when "the word of the Lord was rare") warps the story and creates a misunderstanding concerning the agonizing nature of holy "call." A preacher must deal with the whole story and not just with the sweet part remembered from vacation Bible school. God will affect change by any means possible, even by using an unsuspecting child. But the change will cost something; at least the loss of innocence.

More than in most sermons, I felt it was necessary to give ample background and explore the origins of Samuel's unusual birth. This was partly to set up reflection about our own unusual birth by baptism (this was a marvelous text to follow the preceding week's baptism of our Lord) but also to heighten the narrative tension Samuel felt as a result of his developing relationship with Eli. We are ordained in baptism (the *primary* ordination prior to all clergy hoopla!) but that setting-apart will lead to many agonizing rocks between a plethora of hard places. Young Samuel's divine visitation must have felt like a dark night of the soul.

As with the Joseph story, I found it was necessary in presermon deliberations to read well beyond the limits of the Sunday pericope. We explored in detail the first three chapters of 1 Samuel including the unusual birth, the intimate tutelage between priest and neophyte in the temple, and the scandal (and hilarity) of Eli's wayward sons. We discussed how tightly written the narrative seemed to be and literary issues ranging from irony ("Here I am" the morning after) to tragedy ("Samuel, my son" in light of Eli's worthless boys) in the same verse (3:16). This was the fourth Old Testament lesson in this half of the project. The cumulative effect on the group suggests a recovery of respect for stories long-vilified by moderns.

This sermon was meant to be an extension of the last. When we are brought home from exile it is usually not for vacation but rather *vocation*. Sometimes this call of God (rooted in baptism for the Christian) means that one will stand in a very difficult, Samuel-like place. In short, I wanted listeners to see in Samuel's late-night anguish their own feelings of being stuck between the old and new. Acting on God's call will sometimes bring turbulence among the very voices of caring authority and familial structure that raised a person. Modern prophets, including King, Bonhoeffer, Day, and many others, found themselves precisely in Samuel's uncomfortable place— what to do with divine revelation as they pondered the consequences of being faithful to God and parting ways with mentors who formed them in the faith and now urged them to keep quiet. Was it Rudolf Otto who said that holy ground is defined by the urge to run both toward and away from a burning bush? One group participant put it this way: "While out of the church I passionately believed that 'organized religion' in most cases fostered tradition over positive change. I still do. I feel that for many people the first step is actually out the church door."

This sermon was particularly important for the project group, still struggling (as do all serious Christians) with issues of adult conversion—what one is gaining and what one is leaving behind. I wanted them to *feel* that tension at this point rather than act upon it. Samuel's agonizing, sleepless night is a metaphor for the many nights one faces with conversion that is authentic and ongoing. "I do wonder," said one, "whether" 'judgment day' will in a sense be a weighing of the courage we show in this life." This is fairly good evidence that this particular group member felt some of Samuel's tension. Several in the group mentioned in the evaluation session that they "took leave" of the sermon for awhile to deal with a personal issue, only to tune back in later. I was flattered by this revelation even though they were elsewhere for part of the delivery. They saw their own struggle in Samuel's predicament. This is a main goal for any sermon considering formational concerns.

In our reflections following the sermon, we shared our personal places of Samuel-like agony, but we also discussed our own parish and the transition the congregation recently experienced (I barely alluded to this situation in the sermon—it was enough for that moment). A building project largely left our members either defending the status quo and the past *or* pushing for change, sometimes without much regard to tradition. Eli and Samuel spoke not only to our individual situations but also to our corporate family life.

I asked this post-sermon question in order to measure the group's identification with the bug-eyed child-prophet caught between faithfulness to his old, familiar mentor and the new message borne by an insistent divine voice: "Is God calling you to something new at this point in your spiritual journey?" One responded: " As I sat in a Chinese restaurant [recently], I chanced to read for the thousandth time the trite description of the Ox, who represents my year of birth in the Chinese zodiac—patient, intelligent, slow to anger. All very complimentary. I was feeling pretty good about being an Ox when the downside struck. It takes a two by four across that ample rump just to get his attention. Put her there, Lord! I understand Samuel's feelings maybe more than others. Once while on a business trip, asleep and securely locked in my isolated room, I distinctly heard a voice [say my name] right next to my ear. There were no monsters under the bed. I listened and heard no more. So, I wait. And consider that maybe most of us are only to hear the call given by the gospel and no more. Does it not take greater faith to toil in obscurity than to hear the unmistakable clarion call? Anyway, here I am—dunderhead. Don't even plane down that two by four."

Even though others did have specific areas of newness to share ("I'm going to work harder to reach some of my coworkers who are currently unchurched"; "I feel that God is calling me to a greater sense of calm and confidence after nearly two years of great anxiety over our son's health"), most concurred that they felt a germinating call but were still waiting for clarity and the above two by four. One person admitted: "If God is calling, I'm not hearing and I am trying to listen."

Though I'm fairly sure that this group was not expecting the "clarion call" heard aloud by Samuel, future sermons in this area could probably use a bit more concrete connection to daily life. What does standing between old and new look like for the average person in the pew? One member of the group agreed that many people are faced with a choice that will change everything. "More often, though, we are constantly faced with little decisions which challenge our Christian principles, each dilemma seemingly insignificant." A pastor might profitably spend some time looking at the Samuel text from the lens of an "average" life. Even so, preachers should take care not to overly spell out implications for listeners. They will make their own imaginative connections if given a bit of bread. Under the rubric of "making sure everyone understands," sermons can sometimes squelch the creative process rather than help it along.

Like conversion, God's call is also ongoing and will be sounded insistently until it's heard. Which is to say there are always other Sundays, thankfully, to tackle this most important topic. The sermon succeeded to the extent that my project group could see their lives in Samuel's. That was enough for now. The converted are called. And a call to ministry is both fearful and wondrous.

CHAPTER TWELVE

Learning to Preach from a Pew of Seekers

It was very important for me to try to imagine how new Christians might hear these four texts for the first time. A great danger of preaching is that the preacher assumes too much: that the story is familiar, the narrative flow is clear, and the theology is obvious. Barbara Lundblad believes that creatively retelling a biblical story "may be the most important calling of the preacher in our time."[1] Opening the Bible is ultimately enriching, but initially overwhelming. Preachers forget this over time.

Therefore, my first and primary learning as a result of working with these returnees is not "how" to preach, but how to prepare to preach. Who is listening and why? Where have they come from? What are they looking for? Slipping into the shoes of a newcomer has been an obvious but critical shift that will form my regular Sunday sermons. Given the diversity of a typical Lutheran Sunday assembly, George Hunter (from Asbury Seminary) counseled me to pitch the sermon "primarily at the unconvinced and new converts. Engage their questions and issues from the resources of the gospel, and the seasoned Christian will be able to relate, and their children moreso."[2] If Hunter is right (and I think he is), then a pastor's preaching ministry may greatly benefit from regular, collaborative, small group study with those returning to congregational life. "We were stakeholders in these sermons," one of the seekers in my group excitedly admitted.

What considerations should a preacher entertain in crafting sermons that might reach and even change people returning to church after an absence of some length?

I offer six areas of reflection for others interested in similar work with new Christians:

(1) *Clarifying in-house theological jargon.* Similar to the skeptics group, it is vital that the preacher offer descriptive, vivid examples of theological words that the rest of the congregation largely takes for granted. "Grace," for example, was such a word. Also "call" and "exile." The preacher needs to take special care with image and illustration to connect the gap between theological jargon and lived experience. Poets and novelists are experts when it comes to using a particular concrete image that unlocks universal truths. Reading healthy doses of both has helped my preaching more than any other single discipline. Do not assume that internal visual images from various biblical metaphors readily come to mind for the new listener. They often don't. In fact, try to keep in mind Patrick Henry's student who came to him two weeks into an introductory Bible course and said in despair, "I've been looking everywhere for the footnotes and can't find them." Professor Henry explained: "The only superscript numbers he had previously seen in books were footnote references, so he naturally thought that there must be one for every numbered verse."[3]

(2) *Providing imaginative room for the Holy Spirit.* Use stories to give a new listener the proper emotional "distance" to work on his or her own personal history. You can't slap someone in the face with unvarnished truth. Undistilled, it crushes and overwhelms a person. We either despair under its weight or run from its demands. Lasting insight tends to sneak up on us and surprise by layers. William H. Willimon writes: "The purpose of the church, in great part, is to open the Bible in such a way that it forms an alternative structure of reality among the congregation. People are crushed, frightened, tied in knots, and timid because they have lost their vision, their

imagination. They lack the requisite stories with which to make sense of their lives."[4] A sermon based on a good biblical story, therefore, should never be rushed. Adequate silence should always follow. Avoid the tendency just after the sermon to intone, "Now let us all stand for Hymn #557." Well-timed pauses will give the listener time to find personal intersection in the biblical story as the sermon is delivered. We live in a culture that demands instant meaning with every nuance clearly spelled out. "So we ask, 'What does this text mean to me?' or, more precisely, 'What can I *do* with this text?' before simply sitting quietly and letting the text have its way with us."[5] This is what several group members meant when they reported that they "took leave" of the sermon to consider a personal issue only to "return" later. This is one mark of a successful sermon: not that the preaching is a homiletical masterpiece, but that the text has affected the people on deep levels of meaning. The text, as Karl Barth puts it, should lead a person to "the Word beyond words."

(3) *Allowing listeners to finish the sermon.* For similar reasons, I suggest that sermons aimed at this group attempt an elliptical shape, an unfinished, open-ended, "dot-dot-dot" feel that is to be completed in the minds and hearts of the people. Several members in this group came from a conflicted religious past where authority dictated rigid conformity.[6] Such is the case for many modern returnees. Sermons that are totally explained and wrapped up with an obvious bow will not work well on this group. Authoritarianism is precisely what many returnees fled in an earlier church experience (and what skeptics, by the way, resisted in the opening section). This is not to say that the preacher should abandon basic theological clarity for an "anything goes" style. It is to say that much preaching blunts reflection rather than promoting it. For

many seekers, church has not been associated with words like "discovery" or "journey." Sermons can be an invitation to discover the truth of Christ, rather that force-feeding such truth.

I recall probing around in the book of 2 Kings not long ago, fairly unfamiliar territory for me. Early in that book (6:8-23) is a story about the great prophet Elisha who has angered the King of Aram by spiritually discerning the king's military intentions and passing them on to the king of Israel—some sort of telepathic interception, divinely guided. The Arameans are furious and by night completely surround the city of Dothan, where Elisha is based as he steals these secrets. When morning arrives, one of Elisha's attendants rises early, takes a stroll, and notices that they are completely and hopelessly trapped. "Alas, master! What shall we do?" The prophet seems utterly unconcerned and responds rather strangely given the odds just outside his door: "Do not be afraid, for there are more with us than there are with them." Elisha prays a short morning prayer that his servant "may see." The text then reports: "The Lord opened the eyes of the servant, and he saw; the mountain was full of horses and chariots of fire all around Elisha."

To my knowledge this story does not appear in the Sunday lectionary cycle. But it serves as a good example, nevertheless, of the importance of allowing listeners, even seekers, to finish a biblical story in the imagination of their own lives. In many instances, it is enough to tell the basics of the story and get out of the way. Listeners, however new to church life, will be able to recognize Elisha's predicament and catalog the many ways people have been sent (perhaps by God) to assist in their rescue over the years. Maybe they are not yet ready to confess that the "horses and chariots of fire" on the mountain bear the very saints in light. No matter. The story is at work. One of the main tasks in preaching to seekers is to open only enough of the story so as to help them find intersection in their own lives. God's word will do the rest if we don't kill it by overly offering an "expert" explanation.

(4) *Making connections with the God who "colors outside the lines."* It is vitally important in sermons to help seekers discover that Christians worship a God who is at work well outside of the traditional ecclesiastical boundaries of church life; a God who is wooing the world and active in the life of a seeker long before that person shows up at a church door. It is arrogant to presume that God only emerges upon a seeker's entrance into a church building. Part of the homiletical task is to proclaim the tireless God who loves the entire cosmos (John 3:16) and will go to great and various lengths to help people notice this love. There is a fairly common theology at work among many Christians in this country that goes something like this: "If you believe in Jesus Christ and follow his teachings, then you will be saved. If you do not believe in Jesus, then you are damned to eternal punishment. Jesus loves me this I know, but if I don't love him back, it's to hell I go." The whole point of following Jesus, then, is to make sure your soul is safe for the next life. All other options are not only wrong, they're doomed. Seekers have much in common with skeptics who reject such a narrow understanding of God's work in the world. I love a provocative and timely song from a wonderful off-color country band from Texas called the Lounge Lizards. The song is titled, "Jesus Loves Me, But He Can't Stand You."[7]

The Bible, of course, includes images of judgment for those outside the faith, but also quite regularly paints a different picture. The appearance of King Cyrus, for example, in Isaiah 45 must be problematic and quite troubling for those who draw strict boundaries between those whom God accepts and condemns. King Cyrus, after all, was a non-Israelite. He did not have the Ten Commandments erected on his lawn, did not eat the Seder meal at Passover, and his children did not wear a WWMD ("What Would Moses Do?") bracelet at recess. And yet God has the audacity to call this man "anointed" (45:1), his very chosen one who would help bring Israel back from exile. God seems to be at work in places well outside the prescribed boundaries. "I call you by your name, I surname you, *though you do not know me*" (45:4, italics added). The God of heaven and earth, the God we want to pin down, circumscribe, limit, and confine, chooses an outsider who doesn't even know God's name! In short, this is what we must humbly confess and preach: God colors far outside the lines of our imaginations and is up to far more in this world than we can ever begin to perceive or imagine.

Does this mean Jesus is just the shortstop on God's All-Star team with Buddha at first base, Moses in centerfield, Muhammad catching behind the plate, and Confucius at third? I find that there is very little helpful in trying to amalgamate the religions into one big happy family. Ours is a unique path to God. But to assume that God isn't involved with people until they come to Christ is presumptuous and even contradictory of our own Bible. Cyrus never converted to the Bible's dominant faith, but he was God's anointed nonetheless. Seekers need to hear about the God of love who has been relentlessly pursuing them even before their return to the church, sometimes bringing folk to faith through unconventional means. As Flannery O'Connor once put it: "Most people come to the church by a means that the church does not allow."[8] Preachers need to take time and discover how a seeker arrived at his or her particular congregation and why. Asking these questions (and daring to preach about the answers) might reveal a God who is far bigger than we've ever imagined. "The mission that counts," says Loren Mead, "is God's mission, not the church's. We no longer look at the world for the *gaps*, so that we, in mission, can take God to where God is not now. Instead, we look at the world as the arena in which God's care and love are already, everywhere, at work. We do not take mission out; we go out to meet the mission already there."[9] Faithful proclamation to seekers reveals the God at work in their lives well before the church gets there.

(5) *Preaching between font and table.* With that said (the wideness of God's mercy), it is also important to reveal the Lord who works in particular, sacramental channels of divine love. Every healing bath of baptism reminds us of our own watery death, our origins and peculiar identity. The table of God points to an inclusive feast, hosted by the crucified and resurrected Christ, experienced both now and in the future. All good preaching stands somewhere in between those twin poles upon which the church's tent ministry is pitched. Font and table are fixed. But God's people, undergoing continuing conversion as a result of the radical encounter with God's word, are portable and sent into the world as salt and light. Preaching between font and table has a primary role in seasoning all God's people. This is particularly true for returnees in search of a lost identity. Sermons for this group should also strive to be elliptical in the sacramental sense as well, "to be continued" at the Eucharist or in recalling daily the community's watery entrance into the Body.

I think of the novel *Mr. Ives' Christmas*, which describes the life of a commercial artist in New York City whose son, soon to enter seminary, is murdered on Christmas Day. Though Ives never loses his faith, he certainly wonders about many of the issues that drive people away from church. In many respects he becomes a "seeker" within his own congregation, a man who is searching desperately for meaning and purpose. For years his faith seems dry and arid as he goes through the motions, not sure at times if what he's doing really matters. But most of all, Ives is haunted by a sense of residual guilt as he wonders if he could have done something to prevent the tragedy of his son's death, recounting it in his mind over and over again. In a dream, his son Robert "touched his shoulder and said, 'Pop, why do you keep doing this to yourself?' Then, bending, his hands cupped, his son scooped out a handful of water, and this he poured over his father's head, and then he brought up some more and washed his limbs with that water; and then he was gone."[10] A central theme of this book is how one determined man decides to keep observing the festivals and sacraments of the church long after they've ceased to make much sense, even when he doesn't feel like it. Too much preaching seems to be divorced from this sacramental power. For Mr. Ives, a desperate and disillusioned seeker, such grounding in the church's mysteries was the very thing that reawakened his faith.

Reynolds Price, southern poet and fiction writer who almost died of cancer several years ago, wrote a letter to a young medical student, also facing cancer and mortality. Price wishes that during his own journey of faith more clergy "had forthrightly confronted the silence at the very heart of any God we can worship and that they'd observed it more unflinchingly with us, not dimming our view with rose-colored screens and sweet-voiced chatter that are certain to smash or go cold-dumb at the first touch of heat, not to mention the scalding breath of terror at the sight of pained death."[11] Staying close to font and table keeps the preacher in close touch with death and life's mysteries and steers proclamation away from insincere "sweet-voiced chatter" that a perceptive seeker can detect a mile away.

(6) *Trusting the power of the church year.* Preaching through the seasons of the church year offers a natural time for sermons to raise questions that will appeal to new Christians; questions that regularly surface in the lectionary texts and invite a newcomer into an alternate way of measuring time. *Advent:* What is growing inside of me? *Christmas:* What is being born through me? *Epiphany:* What unique gifts do I bring? *Lent:* What is dying in me? What am I leaving behind? *Easter:* Where is the risen Christ now present in my life? *Pentecost*: What is the Holy Spirit calling me to do and be? "Spend a year with us" is at core an invitation to do business with this powerful calendar. Inherent in the church seasons are timeless biblical issues that powerfully shape a congregational newcomer.

Nora Gallagher, recalling her days as a seeker, writes of Holy Week and how the church year drew her ever more deeply to Christ: "Each service of the Triduum strips away a layer of defensive, outer cells. The whole church is organized in a cycle of seasons, liturgies, holy days, and Gospel readings that may be connected to how life unfolds. We need to revisit our experience over and over again; each time, each visit, another layer is peeled away, another piece or aspect is revealed."[12] A preacher should not feel pressured to squeeze in the "right issue" to impress converts. The lectionary naturally and slowly opens to them in time. In just four sermons this group encountered issues of forgiveness, reconciliation, creation, exile, and call. "This experience has helped me read the Bible more probingly and less dismissively," said one of our seekers. "In the past, I have often viewed the issues or conflicts raised in Bible stories as irrelevant, because they occurred in pre-scientific times. I now focus better on the elements of the stories that transcend time and place." The church year is a great gift providing powerful homiletical structure for pastors preaching with conversion and spiritual formation in mind.

Paul Scott Wilson's words sum up this section for me:

> We begin to conceive of the sermon as an intimate and personal event in a communal context with community-shaping power. It is God's salvation breaking into the world. Consequently our thinking must shift. For instance, we must see that a relationship with God is begun and maintained, not just a relationship with *ideas* about God. When the sermon goes well, information concerning God is not the purpose of the event so much as *God's formation of us in Christ's image*. The sermon we listen to is less an intellectual exercise than it is our being reclaimed by Christ as God's own.[13]

If preaching and ongoing conversion are indeed related, then sermons must focus more on spiritual formation than heady information. The eight gracious people in this test group would support that thesis. In our planning and evaluation sessions, I noticed that these "returnees" to congregational life were not searching primarily for facts about God. For many, it was precisely rigid "facts" that drove them away. Instead, they were searching for the living God who can never be pinned down, the Holy One who imparts transformation and change. Sermons can be a critical, vital part of this ongoing conversion to Christ, the living One who cannot be entombed.

CHAPTER THIRTEEN

A Dream

One of the joys of my work is the opportunity to meet all kinds of people from all walks of life. At parties, social gatherings, school functions, and community meetings, I am drawn into conversation with people about their belief or lack of belief, their "spirituality," or perhaps the most popular topic, "What's wrong with the church today" (read: "Why I'm not part of a congregation"). It's rather surprising how fast these conversations happen and how forthcoming relative strangers are with their feelings. They speak. I usually listen and nod. *The church isn't this; it isn't that . . . I'm disappointed with this, opposed to that . . . The church should be doing more of this, less of that.* Most are not seeking advice, but offering justification for their absence. I'm all ears. This is not a time for pastoral persuasion. They are usually offering both miniconfessional and sturdy defense of their departure. So I listen.

In his book *Why Christian? For Those on the Edge of Faith*, Douglas John Hall writes: "There is no such thing as a 'perfect' church, and the people who go about looking for such an ideal are bound to be disappointed. The Christian gospel isn't about the perfect church, it's about the perfect love of God, which none of us deserves, and from which we all fall short. The church is not a little bit of the world that has finally been fixed up, righted. In a real way, the only thing that distinguishes church and world is that the church knows something about the world that it doesn't usually know about itself: that it is greatly loved."[1]

When I left seminary in 1985, I departed with something of an "activist" model of doing ministry. The church, my assumption went, could not be effective or

faithful unless members radically engaged and transformed the pressing social needs of the day. Indeed, I still
believe that. What was missing as I left seminary was a
sense of God as the primary agent of such change. It
became clear to me one day that the church I envisioned
was not a whole lot different than the local department of
social services or any variety of helping organizations
that work for social justice and community transformation. I began to ask (postseminary): What is the *church's*
unique role and mission in the local community? "The
Christian gospel isn't about the perfect church," Hall
rightly says, "it's about the perfect love of God." And
then I had a rather strange dream.

Not long ago I preached on Acts 17, that wonderful lec-
tion where Paul the convert is waiting (impatiently?) on
Silas and Timothy in Athens. He walks around the city
keeping his eyes open, listening to the latest in Stoic
thought, and reflecting on the abiding attraction of the
local gods (Nike and her "swoosh" perhaps?). Finally, he
can't stand it any longer. He preaches in the middle of the
Areopagus, the only sermon in Acts addressed solely to
Greeks, outsiders to biblical faith.

My sermon on his sermon included a dream I shared
with the congregation that was meant to elicit sympathy
for people who "spend their time in nothing but telling
or hearing something new" (17:21) and are quite conver-
sant in the latest spiritual fad but aren't able to land anywhere theologically. In other words, like many people
coming to our churches, some having given up on church
long ago.

The dream briefly went something like this: I was in a
tree house (my actual home in the dream) and became
aware of an acquaintance down below. I saw him but he
did not see me. He was crying, hard. He walked right
underneath me. I didn't know him very well (we'd

talked at a couple parties), but in my dream I recalled that this was a man who did not believe in God, who had given up on God many years back. When I remembered that about him, I called out and asked what was the matter. He shot me a long glance and said, "Can't you see?! It's my dog. My dog is dead." He was tenderly and slowly pulling his dog around on a leash, but it was lifeless. No bark or breath. He kept looking up at me, as if I could do something about his pet. I've never seen such agony in a person's face. To my shame, which I felt even in the dream, I stayed right where I was, looking down at him from the tree, even grinning a little.

Now all of this may have been the power of suggestion from the plethora of Carl Jung books I'd been reading around that time. Or maybe the following interpretation arose because I'm familiar with the sick joke that goes something like this: "Have you heard the one about the dyslexic atheist who doesn't believe in dogs?" Ha-ha. But in the shower the next morning following this dream, it hit me: what that grieving man was tearfully dragging around on a leash was G-o-d spelled backwards.

I rarely use dreams in a sermon but used parts of this one. I focused on Paul's positive spin on the Athenians' constant searching and dissatisfaction, my (our) typical distance from unbelievers (from a tree looking down), and how I generally wait for hurting people to make appointments. I think the sermon worked on some level. Many liked it.

One of our members, however, an artist who loves God but has major quibbles with the church, smiled and laughed on the way out the door and handed me a folded scrap of notepaper meant for "Little Lutherans" that she'd scavenged from a pew. She is forever handing me these jottings. "Another interpretation," she said. I read it between services. "I think your higher self was musefully looking down at your lower self as that lower self was dragging around another old, no longer functioning image of God that you cared for. Dog = Faithfulness. Growth = Tree. You're in it, Frank. Hold on."

A major problem with using dreams in a sermon: everyone's invited to play "Amateur Analyst," our newest Church Game Show! Come on down! But this note was different. It made some sense. It provided a winsome angle on my dream. Was this more about me than someone else? The relationship of preaching to adult conversion has been a fascinating question for me. But why? Why am I drawn to people outside the church and others just returning while many inside get bogged down with pettiness and a theological shallowness that is sometimes hard to swallow silently? Why were my closest friends in seminary those who decided against ordination? Maybe my artist friend is right. Maybe I'm leaving something behind.

Of this much I'm quite sure: faithful sermons grounded in "the perfect love of God" do not necessarily talk a person into something (say, a theologically orthodox articulation of the second article of the Apostles' Creed) as much as bring something *out* of a person. It's far too much weight on the preacher to expect the former and probably produces the sort of Sunday morning mimicked shallowness that currently frustrates me anyway. Marcus Borg suggests that one of the most pressing needs for modern Christians is to move from what he calls "secondhand religion"[2] (based on believing what one has heard from others or read in a book) to "firsthand religion" (a relationship with the living God to which the Bible, sermons, and church teachings can only point).

Time and again, both groups, even the skeptics, revealed a longing for this firsthand relationship. Fred Craddock, cited earlier in this book, is right. One of the main formational roles of the sermon is to lead a listener along with bits of bread through the woods and help them make their own discoveries. Eventually the "house" the listener rests in is their own, but with a gospel decor. At that point, the sermon, blessedly, is no longer "mine" but has taken off in the imaginations of others. Anne Shirley in *Anne of Green Gables* tells Matthew Cuthbert what she is looking for in a new preacher when the congregation on Prince Edward Island begins their new search and a parade of guest ministers mount the pulpit. "I don't think Mr. Smith would have done, Matthew. Mrs. Lynde says his delivery was so poor, but I think his worst fault was just like Mr. Bentley's—he had no imagination."[3] According to Anne Shirley, a deadly homiletical handicap.

Tapping into the imaginations of listeners instead of handing them a homily prewrapped is an exercise fraught with challenges, chief among them the very real possibility of having ten different listeners offer ten different interpretations of the same sermon (some that are worlds apart!). But the risk is clearly worth it and surely why Jesus, the master preacher, regularly told stories with open endings. We never know if the prodigal and the elder brother reconciled. We don't discover if the man in the ditch is changed by the behavior of the Samaritan. We aren't told if the laborers who worked all day in the vineyard ever resolved their feelings of resentment against those who showed up at the last hour. The framework of the parable gives a listener just enough grist (but not too much) to begin working out the story in his or her own life. In fact, I'm sure many of Jesus' stories detonated in his listeners' lives days after they heard them.

Mark, arguably the earliest Gospel writer, picks up on this idea as he ends his narrative without a real ending

(16:8). The women run from the tomb and say nothing to anybody. In Mark's Easter story, the resurrected Jesus never once appears. There is a *promise* of sight ("He is going ahead of you to Galilee") but nothing like an Emmaus road where Jesus cracks open a fresh loaf of pumpernickel, appears for an instant and then vanishes (Luke 24). Nothing like a morning fish fry on the beach (John 21). There are clear and happy endings in the other Gospels as Jesus gives specific, final directions to his followers who, in some accounts, watch slack-jawed as their Lord rises into heaven. In Mark, however, the ending is rather ambiguous. The story is clearly starting again and the reader is invited to be a character in the plot this time around.[4] Mark ends (begins) his story not with a period but an ellipsis.

For those who may wander into church wondering how they might possibly square their doubts with the ancient claims of the church, it's important to note that at least one storyteller, perhaps the first to describe Easter, wasn't all that interested in our intellectual doubts in the first place—how resurrection could have possibly happened according to the laws of science. Personally, I'd much rather see the Easter Jesus dancing in a field of tulips with Mary Magdalene on the Hallmark Hall of Fame. Mark, apparently, wasn't interested in sightings of a once-dead man. He was more interested in our willingness to give our lives away for others in Christ's name. No wonder the women ran and said nothing. They were next in line for crucifixion—dying for others. With an unclear ending, the story is starting once again and this time we're invited to take part in the drama.

The Sunday sermon, though differing in content given the lectionary text, should often work in precisely this open-ended, parabolic way. The listener is invited into the story of "the perfect love of God" and becomes a real character in the plot. Too much preaching, I fear (including my own), tries to talk the listener into something through a series of compelling, intellectual, theological arguments. This, I'm convinced, doesn't work well with skeptics or seekers.

Jesus was a master at tapping into his listeners' imaginations. Perhaps he knew that this was the primary context where the initial work of conversion had to be waged. This means that preachers (like poets) will tap into that which is universal by getting as concrete as possible, by savoring seemingly inconsequential details of a day, and looking closely at odd twists of the holy peeking out in unexpected places. Several little minidiscoveries, "a series of sips" along the way, lead to a gospel vision that could never be swallowed in the first gulp. A good image works on (and will stay with) a listener quite independently of the proclaimer. Consider: A mustard seed. A lost coin. A woman at a well. An Emmaus walk. A child in a pediatric oncology ward offering his hot bean. A dead turkey. A fire tower. A semiswallowed chipmunk. A tree house. A specific image opens up a whole new world inside the listener. Narnia is as close as the wardrobe upstairs.

How does the God of Life become real again? How do we herald not the perfect community, but instead the perfect love of God? Easter won't happen for a skeptic or seeker or anyone else just because the preacher proclaims it. When Mary Magdalene first found the empty tomb, she originally only thought "missing body" and "local gardener." It was only when Jesus *named* her that Easter happened and her world was transformed. I'm convinced conversion still happens this way, face-to-face, one person at a time. A sermon faces the daunting task of helping a worshiper hear the God of the past and Lord of the future call his or her name in the present. This takes patience, a nonjudgmental preaching stance, and lots of unhurried time. After all, writes Wendy Kaminer, "If you regard faith as a gift, not a choice or achievement, the vilification of nonbelievers seems grossly unfair."[5] (Amen, sister Wendy, a longtime agnostic).

Preachers can never strong-arm or talk someone into faith. Bringing people to faith is not centrally our job in the first place, but the work of the Holy Spirit. One of the primary things we *can* do in sermons is to bring field reports of the ongoing work of said Spirit in the world, share our own experience of Christian discipleship within the faith community, and describe what has happened to others who've followed Jesus on this path long before us. In working with these skeptics and seekers I have learned what an incredible mystery faith really is and how preaching, even though it can never be responsible for conversion, surely has the potential to point a person down the intricate path toward belief and beyond—stirring the water in a deep, deep well whose source and refreshment is the one and holy God. Not a dead God dragged around from the past, but a God alive and unleashed in the world.

It is a great honor and privilege to stand in a long line of proclaimers who dare to speak for God. The healing baptismal waters of which we preach flow from our sanctuaries, bearing God's redeeming word to a thirsty, parched world. Who knows where these waters might go and what lives they might refresh, including many who have given up on God long ago? The power of the prophet's dream and the promise of the healing water beckon the preacher to stand in the pulpit yet another time to speak of the holy mysteries beyond all words, "wherever the river goes":

> Then he brought me back to the entrance of the temple; there, water was flowing from below the

threshold of the temple toward the east (for the temple faced east); and the water was flowing down from below the south end of the threshold of the temple, south of the altar. Then he brought me out by way of the north gate, and led me around on the outside to the outer gate that faces toward the east; and the water was coming out on the south side.

Going on eastward with a cord in his hand, the man measured one thousand cubits, and then led me through the water; and it was ankle-deep. Again he measured one thousand, and led me through the water; and it was knee-deep. Again he measured one thousand, and led me through the water; and it was up to the waist. Again he measured one thousand, and it was a river that I could not cross, for the water had risen; it was deep enough to swim in, a river that could not be crossed. He said to me, "Mortal, have you seen this?"

Then he led me back along the bank of the river. As I came back, I saw on the bank of the river a great many trees on the one side and on the other. He said to me, "This water flows toward the eastern region and goes down into the Arabah; and when it enters the sea, the sea of stagnant waters, the water will become fresh. Wherever the river goes, every living creature that swarms will live, and there will be very many fish, once these waters reach there. It will become fresh; and everything will live where the river goes. (Ezek. 47:1-9)

Notes

Introduction

1. Denise Levertov, "Flickering Mind," in *A Door in the Hive* (New York: New Directions, 1989), p. 64.

2. Mark Collins, "Sightings of Elvis: True Believers." *The Christian Century* (December 15, 1993), p. 1262.

3. Richard Rohr, *Everything Belongs: The Gift of Contemplative Prayer* (New York: The Crossroad Publishing Company, 1999), p. 33.

4. Quoted just before the opening page of John Irving's novel, *A Prayer for Owen Meany* (New York: Ballantine Books, 1989).

5. Kathleen Norris, *Amazing Grace: A Vocabulary of Faith* (New York: Riverhead Books, 1998), p. 63.

6. Nora Gallagher, *Things Seen and Unseen: A Year Lived in Faith* (New York: Alfred A. Knopf, 1998), p. 4.

7. After several years of attending worship, doubts and all, and being welcomed nonjudgmentally by our community, one member of the skeptics group did decide to join the church in May of 2000. Another from this same group has recently started receiving Holy Communion with his family.

8. Barbara Brown Taylor, *The Preaching Life* (Boston: Cowley Publications, 1993), p. 9.

9. Adapted from John Westerhoff, *Bringing Up Children in the Christian Faith* (SanFrancisco: Harper, 1980), pp. 3-4.

10. Gordon Lathrop, *Holy Things: A Liturgical Theology* (Minneapolis: Fortress Press, 1993), p. 171.

11. Michael Heher, "Words to Match" in *Image: A Journal of the Arts and Religion* (Summer 1999), p. 102.

12. Excerpt from Wendell Berry, "Creation Myth" in *A Part* (San Francisco: North Point Press, 1980), p. 45.

SECTION I

Chapter 1. Sermons and the Secular Ear

1. Portions of this section were previously published under the title, "Preaching to a Pew of Agnostics," in *The Christian Ministry* (Nov.-Dec. 1997), pp. 20-23. Used here with permission of the Christian Century Foundation.

2. Doug Duncan, "Kinky: A Texas Jew Boy" in *The Door* (Jan./Feb. 2000), p. 6.

3. Frederick Buechner, *Wishful Thinking: A Seeker's ABC* (SanFrancisco: Harper, 1993), p. 1.

4. For a brief overview of the catechumenal process and its introduction in a local parish setting, see my book, *Percolated Faith: Forming New Adult Christians Through Conversion and Baptism* (Lima, Ohio: CSS Publishing Company, 1996).

5. Peter Berger, *A Far Glory: The Quest for Faith in an Age of Credulity* (New York: Free Press, 1992), p. 18.

6. Annie Dillard, "The Wreck of Time" in *Harper's* magazine (January 1998), p. 55.

7. Frederick Buechner, *Telling the Truth: the Gospel As Tragedy, Comedy and Fairy Tale* (San Francisco: Harper & Row, 1977), p. 37.

Chapter 2: Table Manners in the Kingdom of God

1. Annie Dillard, "The Gospel According to St. Luke," in Alfred Corn, ed., *Incarnation: Contemporary Writers on the New Testament* (New York: Viking, 1990), pp. 26, 35.

2. John F. Alexander, *The Secular Squeeze: Reclaiming Christian Depth in a Shallow World* (Downers Grove, Ill.: InterVarsity Press, 1993), pp. 134, 149.

3. Charles Rice, *The Embodied Word: Preaching as Art and Liturgy* (Minneapolis: Fortress Press, 1991), p. 21.

4. Marva Dawn, *A Royal "Waste" of Time: The Splendor of Worshiping God and Being Church for the World* (Grand Rapids: William B. Eerdmans, 1999), p. 45. Dawn includes several chapters on postmodernism and one on the implications for preaching in a postmodern era.

5. Katherine Paterson, "Why Do You Write for Children?" *Theology Today* (January 2000), pp. 570-71.

6. I do not know the exact source of this quote but am indebted to Ed Davis, professor of geography at Emory and Henry College (Virginia), for passing it along.

Chapter 3. Falling Short

1. Frank G. Honeycutt, "Falling Short," *The Christian Ministry* (Nov.-Dec. 1998), pp. 30-31. Used by permission of The Christian Century Foundation.

2. Adapted from Will D. Campbell, *Forty Acres and a Goat* (San Francisco: Harper & Row, 1986), pp. 187-88.

3. Ted Peters, *Sin: Radical Evil in Soul and Society* (Grand Rapids: William B. Eerdmans, 1994), p. 9.

4. Jack Miles, "Religion Makes a Comeback. (Belief to Follow.)" *The New York Times Magazine* (December 7, 1997), pp. 58-59.

5. Excerpt from Scott Cairns's poem, "A Recuperation of Sin." *Figures for the Ghost* (Athens: University of Georgia Press, 1994), p. 39.

6. Nora Gallagher, *Things Seen and Unseen: A Year Lived in Faith* (New York: Alfred A. Knopf, 1998) p. 180.

7. Ted Peters, *Sin: Radical Evil in Soul and Society*, p. 25.

8. Barbara Brown Taylor, "Preaching Repentance at the Start of a New Millennium," *Journal for Preachers* (Lent 2000), p. 3. Later in this same article, Taylor quotes Paul Tillich in his famous sermon, "You Are Accepted." Tillich argues that the great words of the Christian faith cannot be replaced. "But there *is* a way of rediscovering their meaning the same way that leads us down into the depth of our human existence. In that depth these words were conceived; and there they gained power for all ages; there they must be found again by each generation, and by each of us for himself."

9. *Saving Private Ryan* is a Steven Spielberg film produced by Dreamworks and Paramount Pictures in 1998. Screenplay by Robert Rodat.

10. Walter Brueggemann, *Finally Comes the Poet: Daring Speech for Proclamation* (Minneapolis: Fortress Press, 1989), p. 3.

Chapter 4. Raising Hell or Lowering Heaven?

1. C. S. Lewis, *The Voyage of the Dawn Treader* (New York: Macmillan, 1952), pp. 88-91.

2. Thomas Merton, *The Seven Storey Mountain* (New York: Harcourt Brace Jovanovich, 1948), pp. 222-25.

3. William H. Willimon, *Peculiar Speech: Preaching to the Baptized* (Grand Rapids: William B. Eerdmans, 1992), p. 32.

4. Robert Coles, *Harvard Diary: Reflections on the Sacred and the Secular* (New York: Crossroad, 1988), p. 11.

5. Excerpt from Andrew Hudgins's poem, "Heat Lightning in a

Time of Drought," *The Never-Ending Song* (New York: Houghton Mifflin, 1991), p. 23.

6. Kenneth Untener, *Preaching Better* (Mahwah, N.J.: Paulist Press, 1999). I discovered this quote in Martin E. Marty's *Context* newsletter (Chicago: Claretian Publications, Dec. 1, 1999), p. 7.

7. In their book, *Famous Conversions* (Grand Rapids: William B. Eerdmans, 1983), Hugh T. Kerr and John M. Mulder conclude that "conversion is sometimes a dramatic and clearly identifiable experience, such as Paul's confrontation with Christ on the Damascus road. But it can also be a long and extended process, sometimes with no clear beginning and no clear end. . . . Conversion is not necessarily limited to a radical shift from unbelief or doubt to Christian faith" (xiii-xiv).

Chapter 5. Following a Stranger

1. Romulus Linney, *Jesus Tales* (San Francisco: North Point Press, 1980), p. 85.

2. Shel Silverstein, *Where the Sidewalk Ends* (New York: Harper & Row, 1974), p. 153.

3. Garrison Keillor, "Meeting Donny Hart at the Bus-Stop." From the *Prairie Home Companion* audiotape, "Gospel Birds and Other Stories of Lake Wobegon" (Sides 3 and 4) Minnesota Public Radio, 1985.

4. Peter J. Gomes, chaplain at Harvard, has recently published a wonderfully accessible book for the modern seeker titled *The Good Book: Reading the Bible with Mind and Heart* (New York: William Morrow, 1996). Highly recommended.

5. Walter Brueggemann, "Preaching a Sub-Version" in *Theology Today* (July 1998), p. 195.

Chapter 6. Learning to Preach from a Pew of Agnostics

1. John Updike, "The Future of Faith: Confessions of a Churchgoer" in *The New Yorker* (November 29, 1999), p. 86.

2. Richard John Neuhaus, ed., *The Eternal Pity: Reflections on Dying* (Notre Dame, Indiana: University of Notre Dame Press, 2000), p. 9.

3. Excerpt from Stephen Dunn, *New and Selected Poems 1974–1994* (New York: W. W. Norton, 1994), pp. 183-84.

4. Barbara Brown Taylor, *The Preaching Life* (Boston: Cowley Publications, 1993), p. 7.

5. C. S. Lewis, *The Silver Chair* (New York: Macmillan, 1953), pp. 158-59.

6. Richard Rohr, "Why Does Psychology Always Win? The Process of Conversion from Self-Actualization to Self-Transcendence" in *Sojourners* (November 1991), p. 15.

7. A. G. Harmon, "A Conversation with Doris Betts," *Image: A Journal of the Arts and Religion* (Fall 1995), p. 56.

8. Kathleen Norris, *Amazing Grace: A Vocabulary of Faith* (New York: Riverhead Books, 1998), p. 67.

9. Peter De Vries, *Slouching Towards Kalamazoo* (New York: Penguin Books, 1983), p. 79.

10. Gracia Grindal, "Standing on Promises" in *The Christian Century* (November 13, 1996), p. 1107.

11. Wendy Kaminer, *Sleeping with Extra-Terrestrials: The Rise of Irrationalism and Perils of Piety* (New York: Pantheon Books, 1999), p. 25.

12. Frederick Buechner, *Wishful Thinking: A Seeker's ABC* (San Francisco: Harper, 1993), p. 23.

13. John Alexander, "Embracing Pain" in *The Other Side* (May/June 2000), p. 53.

14. Stephen Chapman, "Is There a God?" *MSN Slate* (September 23, 1996), p. 1.

15. See Peter De Vries's marvelous novel, *The Blood of the Lamb* (New York: Penguin Books, 1961). The main character, Don Wanderhope (there's a name with little theological ambiguity), struggles with the nature of faith through the leukemia and subsequent death of his daughter. The closing chapters are an unforgettable testament to the place of honest and forthright biblical lament in the life of any authentic disciple.

16. David Plotz, "The God of the Gridiron: Does He Care Who Wins the Super Bowl?" *MSN Slate* (February 3, 2000), p. 1.

17. William H. Willimon and Stanley Hauerwas, "Ministry as More Than a Helping Profession," in *The Christian Century* (March 15, 1989) (quoted in *The Christian Ministry*, Nov.–Dec. 1995, p. 36).

SECTION II

Chapter 7. Sermons and the Recently Returned

1. Gary Dorsey, *Congregation: The Journey Back to Church* (New York: Viking Press, 1995), 382.

2. The best I've encountered are: Ann McElligott, *The Catechumenal Process: Adult Initiation and Formation for Christian Life and Ministry* (New York: The Church Hymnal Corporation, 1990); and Elizabeth

O'Connor, *Servant Leaders, Servant Structures* (Washington, D.C.: The Servant Leadership School, 1991), the exciting history of The Church of the Saviour.

3. George Hunter, in his book *How to Reach Secular People* (Nashville: Abingdon Press, 1992), suggests that fully one-third of secular, unchurched people are what he calls "ignostics," people who have "no Christian memory" and "don't know what Christians are talking about" (p. 41).

4. Anthony Trollope, *Barchester Towers* (Ware, Hertfordshire: Wordsworth Classics, 1994), pp. 41-42.

Chapter 8. Payback Time

1. I'm indebted here to Barbara Lundblad and her handout, "Sermon As Magnificat," gleaned from her Doctor of Ministry elective, "On Holy Ground," July 1996.

2. From Lundblad's elective, "On Holy Ground," July 1996.

3. Barbara Brown Taylor, *When God Is Silent* (Boston: Cowley Publications, 1998), pp. 85-86. The author of this quotation is an anonymous friend of Taylor's suggesting a model for preaching.

4. Buechner, *Telling the Truth: The Gospels as Tragedy, Comedy, and Fairy Tale* (San Francisco: Harper & Row, 1977), p. 4. The emphasis here is mine.

Chapter 9. The Cosmic Choir

1. Annie Dillard, *Pilgrim at Tinker Creek* (New York: Bantam Books, 1974), p. 8.

2. Cited in Tom Long's *Preaching and the Literary Forms of the Bible* (Philadelphia: Fortress Press, 1989), p. 45, quoting Laurence Perrine, *Sound and Sense: An Introduction to Poetry* (New York: Harcourt, Brace & World, 1963), p. 24.

3. Jay B. McDaniel, *With Roots and Wings: Christianity in an Age of Ecology and Dialogue* (Maryknoll, N.Y.: Orbis Books, 1995), p. 196.

4. Kathleen Norris, *The Cloister Walk* (New York: Riverhead Books, 1996), p. 204. The story Norris cites is from an unnamed book by Mark Danner. The quotations describing this little girl's bravery are from his account.

Chapter 10. Going Home to God

1. Frederick Buechner, *Telling the Truth: The Gospels as Tragedy, Comedy, and Fairy Tale* (San Francisco: Harper & Row, 1977), pp. 40-41.

2. Barbara Brown Taylor, *When God Is Silent* (Boston: Cowley Publications, 1998), p. 120.

3. Garrison Keillor, "Faith at the Speed of Light" in *Time* (June 14, 1999), p. 252. In this witty response to Gates's assertion, Keillor poses as God and sends a heavenly e-mail: "Beloved Bill: I saw how you allocated your time resources last Sunday morning and was not impressed. Riding a stationary bike? Watching guys on the Men's Channel talk about triglycerides and P.S.A. counts? Three words of advice. Love thy neighbor. Ever hear what happened to the rich man who stiff-armed the beggar Lazarus? I caused a general protection fault, and he has been off-line for centuries."

Chapter 12. Learning to Preach from a Pew of Seekers

1. From Lundblad's elective, "On Holy Ground," July 1996.

2. From letter dated September 6, 1996. Used by permission.

3. Patrick Henry, *The Ironic Christian's Companion: Finding the Marks of God's Grace in the World* (New York: Riverhead Books, 1999), p. 67.

4. William H. Willimon, *What's Right with the Church* (San Francisco: Harper & Row, 1985), p. 99.

5. William H. Willimon, "Postmodern Preaching: Learning to Love the Thickness of the Text," in *Exilic Preaching: Testimony for Christian Exiles in an Increasingly Hostile Culture* (Harrisburg, Penn.: Trinity Press International, 1998), p. 112. In the same article, Willimon makes the interesting observation that while a holy book such as "the Koran has a low tolerance for ambiguity, narrative, enigma, the Bible wallows in it" (p. 108).

6. See Sheri Reynolds' wonderful novel, *The Rapture of Canaan* (New York: Berkley Books, 1995), for a harrowing yet insightful saga of one young woman's experience with an abusive religious community. Asks the main character: "If all things work out in the end, if all things have a purpose, then I wondered if we needed a God at all. Would I go to [Jesus] anyway if I thought he did nothing but watch?" (p. 273). Many people returning to church recall their childhood religious teachers (including parents and preachers) invoking the Bible to excuse myriad abuses in God's name.

7. "Jesus Loves Me (But He Can't Stand You)" is from *Lizard Vision* (1991), recorded by the Lounge Lizards on Flying Fish Records.

8. Kathleen Norris, *Amazing Grace: A Vocabulary of Faith* (New York: Riverhead Books, 1968), p. 270.

9. Loren B. Mead, *Five Challenges for the Once and Future Church* (Bethesda, Md.: The Alban Institute, 1996), p. 73.

10. Oscar Hijuelos, *Mr. Ives' Christmas* (New York: Harper Collins Publishers, 1995), pp. 237-38.

11. Reynolds Price, *Letter to a Man in the Fire: Does God Exist and Does He Care?* (New York: Scribner, 1999), p. 74.

12. Nora Gallagher, *Things Seen and Unseen: A Year Lived in Faith*, p. 126.

13. Paul Scott Wilson, *The Practice of Preaching* (Nashville: Abingdon Press, 1995), p. 23. The emphasis is mine.

Chapter 13. A Dream

1. Douglas John Hall, *Why Christian? For Those on the Edge of Faith* (Minneapolis: Augsburg Fortress, 1998), p. 123.

2. Marcus J. Borg, *Meeting Jesus Again for the First Time: The Historical Jesus and the Heart of Contemporary Faith* (HarperSanFrancisco, 1994), pp. 87-88. Borg credits William James (1902, *The Varieties of Religious Experience*) for the original use of this phrase.

3. L. M. Montgomery, *Anne of Green Gables* (New York: Grosset and Dunlap Publishers, 1908), p. 166.

4. See Ched Myers, *Binding the Strong Man: A Political Reading of Mark's Story of Jesus* (Maryknoll, N.Y.: Orbis Books, 1988), pp. 397-404. Myers goes on to compare Mark with Michael Ende's *The Neverending Story* (London: Penguin Books, 1983), a popular book around our own home which centers on a little boy named Bastian who becomes alienated from his world at school and escapes by immersing himself in the narrative world of a book he is reading. "[Bastian] identifies closely with the book's protagonists, but becomes terrified when it begins to seem that the characters are soliciting *his* help in resolving *their* crisis. Bastian realizes that the story he is reading is doomed unless he responds to its cries for his active involvement. In similar fashion, Mark's narrative of discipleship . . . can continue only if we realize, like Bastian, that we are in fact characters in the very story we thought we were reading. Mark, like Ende's novel, puts the 'future' of the narrative in the hands of the reader" (Myers, p. 449).

5. Wendy Kaminer, *Sleeping with Extra-Terrestrials: The Rise of Irrationalism and Perils of Piety* (New York: Pantheon Books, 1999), p. 39.

For Further Reading

Skeptics and Seekers

Beaudoin, Tom. *Virtual Faith: The Irreverent Spiritual Quest of Generation X.* San Francisco: Jossey-Bass, 1998.

Breech, James. *Jesus and Postmodernism.* Minneapolis: Augsburg Fortress, 1989.

Buechner, Frederick. *Wishful Thinking: A Seeker's ABC.* San Francisco: Harper, 1993.

Covington, Dennis. *Salvation on Sand Mountain: Snake Handling and Redemption in Southern Appalachia.* New York: Addison-Wesley, 1995.

Dillard, Annie. *For the Time Being.* New York: Alfred A. Knopf, 1999.

Dorsey, Gary. *Congregation: The Journey Back to Church.* New York: Viking, 1995.

Gallagher, Nora. *Things Seen and Unseen: A Year Lived in Faith.* New York: Alfred A. Knopf, 1998.

Glynn, Patrick. *God the Evidence: The Reconciliation of Faith and Reason in a Postsecular World.* Rocklin, Calif.: Prima Publishing, 1997.

Gould, Stephen Jay. *Rocks of Ages: Science and Religion in the Fullness of Life.* New York: Ballantine Books, 1999.

Grenz, Stanley J. *A Primer on Postmodernism.* Grand Rapids: William B. Eerdmans, 1996.

Hall, Douglas John. *Why Christian? For Those on the Edge of Faith.* Minneapolis: Augsburg Fortress, 1998.

Henry, Patrick. *The Ironic Christian's Companion: Finding the Marks of God's Grace in the World.* New York: Riverhead Books, 1999.

Hoge, Dean R., Benton Johnson, and Donald A. Luidens. *Vanishing Boundaries: The Religion of Mainline Protestant Baby Boomers.* Louisville: Westminster/John Knox, 1994.

Honeycutt, Frank G. "The Lure of Express Conversion." In *What Do You Seek? Welcoming the Adult Inquirer*, pp. 15-23. Edited by Dennis Bushkofsky. Minneapolis: Augsburg Fortress, 2000.

Hunter, George G. III. *How to Reach Secular People*. Nashville: Abingdon Press, 1992.

Kaminer, Wendy. *Sleeping with Extra-Terrestrials: The Rise of Irrationalism and Perils of Piety*. New York: Pantheon Books, 1999.

Kerr, Hugh T., and John M. Mulder, eds. *Famous Conversions: The Christian Experience*. Grand Rapids: William B. Eerdmans, 1994.

Lamott, Anne. *Traveling Mercies: Some Thoughts on Faith*. New York: Pantheon Books, 1999.

McDaniel, Jay B. *With Roots and Wings: Christianity in an Age of Ecology and Dialogue*. New York: Orbis Books, 1995.

Mandelker, Amy, and Elizabeth Powers, eds. *Pilgrim Souls: An Anthology of Spiritual Autobiographies*. New York: Touchstone, 1999.

Mead, Loren B. *Five Challenges for the Once and Future Church*. Bethesda, Maryland: The Alban Institute, 1996.

_______. *The Once and Future Church: Reinventing the Congregation for a New Mission Frontier*. Bethesda, Maryland: The Alban Institute, 1991.

Neuhaus, Richard John, ed. *The Eternal Pity: Reflections on Dying*. Notre Dame, Indiana: University of Notre Dame Press, 2000.

Norris, Kathleen. *Amazing Grace: A Vocabulary of Faith*. New York: Riverhead Books, 1998.

_______. *The Cloister Walk*. New York: Riverhead Books, 1996.

Nouwen, Henri J. M. *Letters to Marc about Jesus*. San Francisco: Harper & Row, 1987.

Peters, Ted. *The World's Future: Systematic Theoloy for a New Era*. Minneapolis: Fortress Press, 2000.

Peters, Ted. *Sin: Radical Evil in Soul and Society*. Grand Rapids: William B. Eerdmans, 1994.

Price, Reynolds. *Letter to a Man in the Fire: Does God Exist and Does He Care?* New York: Scribner, 1999.

Tickle, Phyllis A. *God-Talk in America*. New York: Crossroad Publishing, 1997.

Wakefield, Dan. *Returning: A Spiritual Journey*. New York: Penguin Books, 1984.

Preaching

Brueggemann, Walter. *Finally Comes the Poet: Daring Speech for Proclamation*. Minneapolis: Augsburg Fortress, 1989.

Buechner, Frederick. *Telling the Truth: The Gospel as Tragedy, Comedy, and Fairy Tale*. San Francisco: Harper & Row, 1977.

For Further Reading

Clarke, Erskine, ed. *Exilic Preaching: Testimony for Christian Exiles in an Increasingly Hostile Culture.* Harrisburg, Penn.: Trinity Press International, 1998.

Craddock, Fred B. *Preaching.* Nashville: Abingdon Press, 1985.

Long, Thomas G. *Preaching and the Literary Forms of the Bible.* Philadelphia: Fortress Press, 1989.

Rice, Charles L. *The Embodied Word: Preaching as Art and Liturgy.* Minneapolis: Augsburg Fortress, 1991.

Taylor, Barbara Brown. *When God Is Silent.* Boston: Cowley Publications, 1998.

_____. *The Preaching Life.* Boston: Cowley Publications, 1993.

Willimon, William H. *The Intrusive Word: Preaching to the Unbaptized.* Grand Rapids: William B. Eerdmans, 1994.

_____. *Peculiar Speech: Preaching to the Baptized.* Grand Rapids: William B. Eerdmans, 1992.

Wilson, Paul Scott. *The Practice of Preaching.* Nashville: Abingdon Press, 1995.

Christian Formation

Alexander, John F. *The Secular Squeeze: Reclaiming Christian Depth in a Shallow World.* Downers Grove, Ill.: InterVarsity Press, 1993.

Cosby, N. Gordon. *By Grace Transformed: Christianity for a New Millennium.* New York: Crossroad Publishing, 1999.

Dawn, Marva J. *A Royal "Waste" of Time: The Splendor of Worshiping God and Being Church for the World.* Grand Rapids: William B. Eerdmans, 1999.

Mulholland, M. Robert Jr. *Invitation to a Journey: A Road Map for Spiritual Formation.* Downers Grove, Ill.: InterVarsity Press, 1993.

O'Connor, Elizabeth. *Servant Leaders, Servant Structures.* Washington, D.C.: The Servant Leadership School, 1991.

Willard, Dallas. *The Divine Conspiracy: Rediscovering Our Hidden Life in God.* SanFrancisco: Harper, 1998.

_____. *The Spirit of the Disciplines: Understanding How God Changes Lives.* SanFrancisco: Harper, 1988.

Yancey, Philip. *I Was Just Wondering.* Grand Rapids: William B. Eerdmans, 1989.

Fiction

Betts, Doris. *Souls Raised from the Dead.* New York: Scribner, 1994.

_____. *The Sharp Teeth of Love.* New York: Alfred A. Knopf, 1997.

For Further Reading

De Vries, Peter. *The Blood of the Lamb*. New York: Penguin Books, 1961.

Endo, Shusaku. *Silence*. New York: Taplinger Publishing, 1969.

Frederic, Harold. *The Damnation of Theron Ware*. Amherst, N.Y.: Prometheus Books, 1896.

Hansen, Ron. *Atticus*. New York: Harper Collins, 1996.

———. *Mariette in Ecstasy*. New York: Harper Collins, 1991.

Hijuelos, Oscar. *Mr. Ives' Christmas*. New York: Harper Collins, 1995.

Irving, John. *A Prayer for Owen Meany*. New York: Ballantine Books, 1989.

Kingsolver, Barbara. *The Poisonwood Bible*. New York: Harper Collins, 1998.

O'Connor, Flannery. *The Complete Stories*. New York: Farrar, Straus and Giroux, 1984.

Rash, Ron. *The Night the New Jesus Fell to Earth and Other Stories from Cliffside, North Carolina*. Columbia, S.C.: The Bench Press, 1994.

Reynolds, Sheri. *The Rapture of Canaan*. New York: Berkley Books, 1995.

Roth, Philip. *American Pastoral*. New York: Houghton Mifflin, 1997.

Tyler, Anne. *Saint Maybe*. New York: Alfred A. Knopf, 1991.

Updike, John. *In the Beauty of the Lilies*. Alfred A. Knopf, 1996.

Poetry

Cairns, Scott, *Recovered Body*. New York: George Braziller, Inc., 1998.

Dunn, Stephen. *New and Selected Poems 1974–1994*. New York: W. W. Norton and Company, 1994.

Hudgins, Andrew. *After the Lost War: A Narrative*. New York: Houghton Mifflin, 1988.

———. *The Glass Hammer: A Southern Childhood*. New York: Houghton Mifflin, 1994.

———. *The Never-Ending*. New York: Houghton Mifflin, 1991.

Powell, Lynn. *Old and New Testaments*. Madison: The University of Wisconsin Press, 1995.

Rash, Ron. *Among the Believers*. Oak Ridge, Tenn.: Iris Press, 2000.

Shaw, Luci. *Writing the River*. Colorado Springs, Co.: Pinon Press, 1994.